Transforming Student Ministry

[Research Calling for Change]

RICHARD ROSS

General Editor

LifeWay Press®
Nashville, Tennessee

ISBN: 1415825963
Dewey Decimal Classification Number: 259.23
Subject Heading: Teenagers—Religious Life/Student Ministries/Church
Work with Students

Printed in the United States of America

Student Ministry Publishing
LifeWay Church Resources
One LifeWay Plaza
Nashville, Tennessee 37234-0174

Table of Contents

The Writers 4

Foreword, *Richard Ross* 5

Introduction, *Christian Smith*..10

CHAPTER 1: Raising Up Kingdom Teenagers, *Ken Hemphill*....................13

CHAPTER 2: Scripture and Kingdom Parenting, *Ken Hemphill* 23

CHAPTER 3: Who Teenagers Think God Is, *Rick Morton*.........................31

CHAPTER 4: Introducing Teenagers to God, *Tom Wilks*........................... 41

CHAPTER 5: The Adults Teenagers Need

    The Research, *Roger Glidewell* 54

    The Implications, *Mike Landrum* 65

CHAPTER 6: Impacting Teenagers at Home

    The Research, *Wes Black*.. 77

    The Implications, *Phil Briggs* 89

CHAPTER 7: Impacting Teenagers at Church

    The Research, *Brian Richardson*...103

    The Implications, *Karen Jones*.. 117

EPILOGUE: Releasing Teenagers to the Kingdom, *Richard Ross*............... 132

PARENT REVIVAL AND TEACHING SUGGESTIONS,

    Walter Norvell and Richard Ross.. 145

APPENDIX ONE: A Dream for Impacting Teenagers and

    Their Families, *Richard Ross* 159

APPENDIX TWO: Family Dedication at the Birth of a Baby

    Richard Ross.. 160

The Writers

Dr. Richard Ross is professor of student ministry at Southwestern Baptist Theological Seminary in Fort Worth, TX.

Dr. Christian Smith is the Stuart Chapin distinguished professor of sociology and associate chair of the sociology department at the University of North Carolina at Chapel Hill. He also is principle investigator for the National Study of Youth and Religion.

Dr. Ken Hemphill is the national strategist for Empowering Kingdom Growth for the Southern Baptist Convention in Nashville, TN.

Dr. Rick Morton serves as assistant professor of Christian education and the associate director of the Youth Ministry Institute at the New Orleans Baptist Theological Seminary in New Orleans, LA.

Dr. Tom Wilks is the Jewell and Joe Huitt professor of religious education, professor of applied ministry, and the director of in-service guidance at Oklahoma Baptist University in Shawnee, OK.

Roger Glidewell leads Global Youth Ministry, a youth ministry leadership organization, and is associate professor of youth ministry at Union University, Jackson, TN.

Mike Landrum serves as the director of youth ministry at North Greenville College in Tigerville, SC.

Dr. Wes Black is professor of student ministry and associate dean for PhD studies, School of Educational Ministries, Southwestern Baptist Theological Seminary, Fort Worth, TX.

Dr. Phil Briggs is the retired distinguished professor of collegiate and student ministry at Southwestern Baptist Theological Seminary in Fort Worth, TX.

Dr. Brian Richardson is the Basil Manly, Jr. professor of leadership and church ministry at The Southern Baptist Theological Seminary in Louisville, KY.

Dr. Karen Jones is associate professor of educational leadership at Golden Gate Baptist Theological Seminary in Mill Valley, CA, and associate professor of ministry and missions at Huntington University in Huntington, IN.

Dr. Walter Norvell is assistant professor of Christian education at Midwestern Baptist Theological Seminary in Kansas City, MO.

Foreword

Richard Ross

THE SUBTITLE OF THIS BOOK is interesting—"Research Calling for Change." This raises the question: What research?

The professors who wrote the following chapters do call for significant change in the homes of Christian families and in local church student ministries, but their rationale for calling for change is not based on hunches. Instead, their chapters are grounded in credible research. The authors draw from many important studies related to teenagers and families, but one study receives special focus.

The recently completed National Study of Youth and Religion has profound implications for the church and the home. At many points, the study refutes hunches that many have had about the religious lives of teenagers in recent years. In fact, the study contradicts the conclusions of some informal surveys of teenagers that many church leaders have accepted as fact.

Church leaders and parents who read this book will discover conclusions that fly in the face of conventional wisdom. They will see glaring inconsistencies between what we now know about teenagers and how we work with them at home and church. In summary, they will find "research calling for change."

Dr. Christian Smith is a research scientist and the lead researcher with the National Study of Youth and Religion (NSYR). He has provided a helpful overview of this landmark study in the introduction that follows. In addition, page numbers from his recent work, *Soul Searching: The Religious and Spiritual Lives of American Teenagers* (Oxford University Press: 2005), are referenced in parentheses throughout this book. More information about the study and its findings may be gained from the NSYR Web site at *www.youthandreligion.org*.

For the purposes of *Transforming Student Ministry*, here are several of the most important conclusions coming from Dr. Smith and his research team. Without any doubt, this is research calling for change. (Each of the following conclusions will be discussed at length in the chapters that follow, with references to original sources for the National Study of Youth and Religion.)

CONVENTIONAL WISDOM. Teenagers as an age group are similar to each other in most areas, including their religious thoughts and lives.

NSYR. *There is tremendous variance among teenagers. They vary in religious commitment, beliefs, experiences, and practices, ranging from intense religious involvement and devotion to complete disconnection from religion.*

CONVENTIONAL WISDOM. The teenage years usually are marked by movement away from religion and religious participation.

NSYR. *Teenagers are religiously quite active in a variety of ways, including large minorities and sometimes majorities who claim religious identities and participate in some form of congregational life.*

CONVENTIONAL WISDOM. Teenagers typically rebel against their parents and other adults in their lives and thus reject the faith of those adults.

NSYR. *The lives and faith of most teenagers closely reflect the lives, faith, culture, and institutional settings of the adult world they inhabit. They are only superficially distinct from or rebellious to the adult world. By the time they reach their twenties, most teenagers will be almost identical to their parents in terms of faith and religious practice.*

CONVENTIONAL WISDOM. Teenagers raised in Christian homes and the church have a pretty fair understanding of their religious beliefs.

NSYR. *The vast majority of teenagers are incredibly inarticulate about faith and practices, and its meaning or place in their lives. They find it almost impossible to put basic beliefs into words.*

CONVENTIONAL WISDOM. Church teenagers are aware that their faith and religious practice have been shaped by their homes and churches.

NSYR. *Teenagers are profoundly individualistic and they believe they have developed their faith and practices almost entirely on their own. They do not say their* religious upbringing influences them because they do not really believe anything influences them.

CONVENTIONAL WISDOM. Church teenagers understand that they exist for the glory of God.

NSYR. *Teenagers assume an instrumental view of religion. Religion exists to help individuals be and do what they want. They do not relate to an external faith that makes compelling claims or demands on their lives, especially when it comes to changing and growing in ways they see as inconvenient or uncomfortable.*

CONVENTIONAL WISDOM. Church teenagers understand that God is intimately involved in every facet of their daily lives.

NSYR. *Teenagers are "functional deists." They believe God exists, created the world, and set life in motion. They do not view God as particularly involved in the world's affairs or their own personal lives in a meaningful way, though. In their minds, the only time He becomes involved with them in a personal way is to make their lives happier or to solve some problem.*

CONVENTIONAL WISDOM. Church teenagers have resisted the influence of those who want them to be politically correct and "tolerant" in all their religious conversations.

NSYR. *Teenagers are incredibly well-trained in using "correct" language so they will not offend anyone in public. Away from church they cannot bring themselves to say that Jesus is the only way to God.*

CONVENTIONAL WISDOM. Evangelical teenagers have a fairly good understanding of grace and the basics of salvation.

NSYR. *There is strong evidence that many evangelical teenagers do not understand grace or the basics of salvation.*

CONVENTIONAL WISDOM. Church families recognize the value of church life for children and therefore make it a high priority in terms of family schedules.

NSYR. *The church operates in a social-structurally weak position, competing for time, energy, and attention. It often loses that competition against other more dominant demands and commitments, particularly against school, television, and other media.*

CONVENTIONAL WISDOM. Teenagers in the church are no different than teenagers out in the community.

NSYR. *Despite its weaknesses and lack of influence, religious practice does indeed make a clear significant difference across all standard measurable outcomes in adolescents' lives. It also makes an observable difference in the quality of teen's lives, in the degree to which they are involved in at-risk behaviors, and in their commitment to positive practices.*

CONVENTIONAL WISDOM. Teenagers are getting good teaching at home and church.

NSYR. *American teens are eminently teachable and desperately need teaching. When it comes to a number of things (school, sports, health), there is direct instruction. When it comes to things of the faith, however, parents and leaders have failed to teach clearly.*

Groundbreaking research can provide new insights for leaders and parents as they join God in the spiritual transformation of the next generation.

Parent Revivals

The primary goal of teenagers must be to use their gifts and resources to advance God's kingdom so that every tribe, nation, and people group has the opportunity to respond to their rightful King. To achieve this purpose, teenagers must obey God's Word and embody His name, thus reflecting His character. That also must be the goal of Christian parenting and student ministry.

This book has two purposes. The first is to stimulate church leaders, and especially student leaders, to consider new research that may lead to change. Powerful research emerging in recent days can and probably will lead to a redesign of church student ministry. That same research can and probably will lead to change in Christian homes with teenagers.

The second purpose of this book is to serve as preparation for church leaders who will train and impact parents. This book contains both the background information and the teaching suggestions for leaders who want to train parents in their roles as spiritual leaders.

The companion to this book is the book *Parenting with Kingdom Purpose* by Ken Hemphill and Richard Ross. During training, *Transforming Student Ministry: Research Calling for Change* can serve as a leader book while *Parenting with Kingdom Purpose* serves as the pupil book.

Both books can be used as pastors and church leaders coordinate what might be called a "parent revival." For leaders interested in this approach, a teaching plan can be found on pages 145-158. The plan is built around four events: Sunday School, morning worship, evening worship, and parent revival banquet. Of course, leaders are encouraged to adapt this plan to fit whatever time frame they have available.

Church leaders who follow the parent revival plan will use an entire Sunday to call parents to return to their biblical responsibilities within the home and to give those parents the primary tools they need to impact their children for the kingdom. The four powerful events described on pages 145-158 will equip pastors and church leaders who believe the issue of parenting in our day demands attention from the pulpit. Because services on Sunday should include music, family testimonies, and other elements, pastors and leaders will not be able to address all the complexities of kingdom parenting. They will want each parent in the congregation to have a copy of *Parenting with Kingdom Purpose* in order to flesh out the inspiration and general direction they receive from the pulpit.

Introduction

Christian Smith

WHAT IS THE National Study of Youth and Religion (NSYR) and why should readers pay attention to its findings? In short, the NSYR is the most extensive and detailed national research study on the religious and spiritual lives of U.S. teenagers to date, providing a depth of knowledge and understanding about the religious lives of U.S. adolescents that simply was not available previously. Such knowledge and understanding provide a good basis for informed reflection and discussion in many communities—including communities of faith—concerned with the lives of teenagers in the United States today.

In 2000, while considering the idea of studying adolescent religion in the U.S., I was surprised to discover how little reliable research had been conducted on youth religion at a national level. I came across some existing surveys about teenage religion with relative small samples and methodologies that seemed questionable. I also found some good general adolescent surveys, but they only included a few questions about religion. In the end, it seemed nobody had as much broad social scientific knowledge about the religious and spiritual lives of U.S. teenagers as I had expected would be available and as many people's apparent interest in the matter seemed to warrant.

In response to that lack of knowledge, the Lilly Endowment, Inc. generously granted an award to conduct a national research study of U.S. adolescent religion, giving birth to the NSYR (*www.youthandreligion. org*). In the spring and summer of 2003, after a year and a half of preparation, the NSYR conducted a national telephone survey with 3,370 teen-parent pairs from around the United States. Respondents were chosen with a random-digit-dialing method, assuring a nationally representative sample of teens and their parents. In each case, a 30-minute (average) survey was conducted with one parent and a 52-minute (average) survey was conducted with a teenager randomly chosen from the household.

The survey—which was conducted in English and Spanish, as needed—gathered an immense amount of information on U.S. teenagers' religious affiliations, beliefs, identities, experiences, practices, commitments, activities, congregations, and expected futures. The survey also collected a large amount of data about the teens' families, relationships with parents, schools, friends, neighborhoods, moral attitudes and actions, risk behaviors, dating and sexual experiences, emotional well-being, social ties to adults, and much more. No other existing national survey of teenagers comes close to having the detail of information on these aspects of American adolescents' lives, particularly their religious lives, as the NSYR contains.

In order to follow up on the telephone survey with a complementary research methodology, members of the NSYR research team conducted personal, in-depth interviews with 267 teens from 45 different states, sampled from among the survey respondents. These 267 interview subjects were sampled to achieve diversity of religious type, regional location, gender, age, race, school type, and family structure background.

In these interviews—conducted privately and confidentially, mostly in libraries and restaurants in their hometowns—teens were able to describe and explain their religious faith, spiritual practices, life experiences, thoughts, beliefs, feelings, and hopes in much greater depth than they could on the survey. In these interviews, we were able to gain a much deeper nuance of understanding of the teens' lives, yet the information from their answers connected back to their original survey answers. This provided a direct link between quantitative and qualitative data. (For details on the survey and interview methodologies, see *http://www.youthandreligion.org/research.*)

The broad scope and scale of the NSYR's effort in researching the religious and spiritual lives of U.S. teenagers is unprecedented and has the potential to be highly informative for a variety of people and groups interested in the lives of adolescents. The survey and interview data together provide a wealth of information on an enormous variety of subjects, all connected to a new and unparalleled body of nationally-representative research data on teenagers' religious and spiritual lives.

As a result, scholars are now able to use solid evidence to test their prior observations, evaluate their hypotheses, confirm their hunches, and generally expand the body of reliable knowledge about U.S. adolescents' lives. Persons and communities of faith should thus be better able to understand their own teenagers and to work on more well-informed relationships with the teens in their midst. The stronger relationships then can lead to more effective practices and programs designed to meet teens' religious and spiritual needs.

The NSYR does not exist to tell people what to do with its findings. It is the job of the users—and not the providers—of sociological research to consider what findings may mean in their particular situations. The NSYR exists rather to provide reliable sociological data and findings to a variety of interested users, and to support informed and hopefully constructive conversations about teenagers' real lives.

Clearly, among faith communities in the United States, the implications of the NSYR findings will vary from one faith tradition, denomination, or congregation to another. For those parents, communities, and organizations concerned with the lives of U.S. adolescents—particularly those who deal with their religious and spiritual lives—the NSYR offers a wealth of new and reliable information to dig into, contemplate, discuss, and respond to. We hope that, in the end, NSYR findings contribute to improved relationships and lives in a variety of settings for U.S. teenagers and for those responsible for their well-being.

CHAPTER ONE

Raising Up Kingdom Teenagers

Ken Hemphill

I HAVE BEEN ENCOURAGED to note that various voices are asking parents to take a more active role in the lives of their teenagers. Television commercials pose the question, "Do you know where your child is tonight?" We are being encouraged to ask tough questions about drugs and premarital sex. These are all good and pertinent issues about which every parent and youth leader should be concerned. 13

A More Critical Question

But there is another line of questions that points to a more critical issue of concern that we are not being told to ask our teenagers. Let me pose this question in several different ways. These next questions may be the most important questions any youth leader can teach parents to ask their child or themselves.

- Are you raising a potential teenage deist?
- Do you know what that means? Would you be aware if the signs were present?
- Do you care? Do you care enough? Does your child know you care?
- Do you know what your child believes?
- Have you asked him or her?
- Does your child know what you believe?
- Have you told him or her?
- Perhaps more importantly—have you shown him or her?

Would the teenagers in your church say, "The kingdom of God is the overwhelming concern for my parents as well as my leaders?" Do teenagers know that their parents would rather they make an impact for the kingdom of God than any other single accomplishment in life?

Troubling and Encouraging

I am almost certain this book will be at once the most troubling and most encouraging book you may have ever read. In truth, it is not a book to be read, but one to be mulled over and then acted upon. It may be one of the most critical books of our time for one reason only. If we fail to hand to the next generation a vibrant, kingdom-focused faith, we could see the tragedy of churches that become a respected part of the landscape of American culture, a sort of historic relic of the past, but with little vitality or relevance for the modern-day America.

The greatest need of our day is that we instill in the parents and leaders of our teenagers a passion for the kingdom of God. This single passion, when fully understood, will unify all they do at church and at home. It also will help them nurture teenagers who will strive for excellence in every other aspect of their lives so they can advance the kingdom.

The greatest threat to kingdom impact is that our kids may grow up to imitate and duplicate our own level of kingdom commitment. Most teenagers raised in Christian homes don't rebel against the faith; they just don't think it is a big deal. For most of our teenagers, God is OK—as long as He exists to make me happy and will stay in the background until I need Him.

Even as I mention this concern, I pray it is not true for you or me. I pray that the very fact that you are holding this book suggests that you want to prioritize the kingdom, and you desire to work with the parents of your teenagers to help them to develop kingdom-focused teenagers. But it is true that our teenagers often mirror our level of commitment.

The greatest hope we have is that we now know what is at stake as it relates to kingdom focus and that there is still time to do something about it. We are hopeful because the Father seems to be moving His body to focus on His kingdom. We are hopeful because you are reading this book. Could it be that the Father has given us a wake-up call before it is too late? Will you take the challenge to partner with kingdom parents to raise up kingdom-empowered teenagers?

It Couldn't Happen Here!

Think it couldn't happen? Do you think it is not possible that Christian faith could become little more than a faint historical reference in our country? Take a glimpse across the Atlantic to Great Britain. This nation was once the heart of evangelical Christianity. It was the mission-sending center of the world. Much of London once waited with bated breath to see the latest installment of Spurgeon's sermon, which was featured in the newspaper. Spurgeon and other great expositors preached to packed houses on Sundays.

Today the great churches and cathedrals of England are often little more than monuments, tourist attractions that bear a woeful testimony to a day long passed when revival sparked mission passion. Missions and evangelism are no longer the heartbeat of this nation and some statisticians indicate that less than two percent of the population of England attend church on a given Sunday morning.

Let me add a parenthetical comment. There are pockets of awakening and revival in Great Britain today. I have been privileged to attend British churches where the Spirit of the Lord is powerfully present. I have been thrilled to see teenagers packing houses of worship on Sunday evenings. But sadly, that is still the exception rather than the rule in far too many instances. Beyond that, most missiologists who look at this once great evangelical center would agree that an entire generation was somehow missed.

For the sake of the kingdom, we cannot afford to miss a generation. Too much is at stake. If we lose our kingdom focus, God will use another nation to advance His kingdom. God's kingdom will be victorious! His kingdom is not at risk! But it is possible that we will not be a vital part in His kingdom advance. If this becomes reality, then our culture will plummet into secularism.

This book is a mandate for churches and families to work together to ensure that we remain a vital force for the expansion of the kingdom. It is a wake-up call that we must heed.

The Kingdom-Focused Parent

What would you say is the number one priority of the parents of the teenagers of your church? Would the teenagers agree with your assessment? Perhaps you think I am being a bit too inquisitive with all the questions or perhaps you think I am being a bit of an alarmist. I will plead guilty on both counts.

I believe that parenting has ramifications that are more far-reaching than previously imagined. In the nurturing and discipling of teenagers, parents have the opportunity not only to have a profound impact on the lives of their teenagers, but they also have the challenge to transform the world and to have an impact for eternity. If you think this is a vast overstatement, you may not have fully grasped the significance of the kingdom of God.

If you haven't yet read *Empowering Kingdom Growth: The Heartbeat of God*, I would highly recommend it to you as a companion to this work. It lays the biblical foundation for understanding the priority of the kingdom. You might want to use the 40-day study to assist parents in developing a kingdom focus for their homes.

Once parents understand that only two kingdoms exist—the kingdom of this world, which is destined to pass away, and the kingdom of God, which is eternal—the mandate becomes to instill in our teenagers a passion for God's kingdom. When parents are led to understand that God created each child unique so that he or she could serve His own purpose, then the number one goal of the parent should be to lead each child into an intimate and growing relationship with the Lord so that each child will discover his or her role in advancing God's kingdom.

Jesus the Teenager

If you question whether such an approach will produce a well-rounded and successful teenager, I invite you to look at the greatest example of faith—Jesus. We are told: *"And Jesus increased in wisdom and stature, and in favor with God and with people"* (Luke 2:52). Most of us are familiar with this oft-quoted text. But are you equally familiar with the context?

When He was 12 years old, Jesus had been brought to the temple in Jerusalem. His parents had headed home assuming He was in their extended traveling party. When they realized that He was missing, they returned to find Him. After days of searching, they found Him in the temple sitting among the teachers. Immediately after this section we are told: *"Then He went down with them and came to Nazareth and was obedient to them"* (Luke 2:51).

There is a clear connection between Jesus' obedience to His earthly parents and His development. Joseph and Mary provided the nurture that enabled Jesus to grow intellectually, physically, spiritually, and socially. Don't forget that Jesus' development had a single purpose in mind—that He might fulfill His purpose in advancing God's kingdom.

We also see this in His preaching and His praying. When we look at the prayer of Jesus in Matthew 6:9-13, we see this intentionality. There is nothing trite or selfish about this prayer. He does not see prayer as a means of manipulating the Father, nor does He seek the expansion of His own kingdom. He asks only that the Father's name be glorified through His life, that His kingdom be advanced by His life, and that His Father's will be accomplished in His life.

Truth be told, the commitment of Jesus to the directives of this prayer would one day lead to a death sentence. Remember, for the Father's kingdom to be advanced, it was necessary for His Son to die for the sins of all humanity. Are the parents of your teenagers willing to let their children's lives be expended to advance the kingdom? Do your teenagers know this?

Releasing Teenagers to Risk

I know that this is not easy reading. I understand that this is where the proverbial rubber meets the road. You may be thinking, *I am not sure the parents I work with are willing to see their children called to a mission post that would put them at risk.* This is where the church and the home must work in partnership to develop kingdom commitment.

I was speaking at a Christian conference center recently on the priority of the kingdom. When I finished the message, I was approached by two ladies. One's face was radiant; the other was etched with fear and pain. The young lady with the radiant face excitedly told me of her decision to go to seminary. By now, I had surmised that the lady whose face was etched with fear was the mother. When her twenty-something daughter bounded off to join her friends, she looked at me and whined. "I don't think I can let her go. I am so afraid I'll lose her."

How can you lose someone when you place them in God's hands?

How Parents Define Success

How will the parents you work with determine whether their child's life is a success? How will they measure it? Will it be measured in grades, trophies, job security, size of home, or some other worldly assessment? None of these things are necessarily wrong in and of themselves. They are simply not an adequate measure of the quality of life when one truly understands the priority of the kingdom.

Do the teenagers in your ministry understand the true meaning of success from a biblical standpoint? Do you enforce this perspective by your affirmation? Do you help parents develop this perspective on life?

It appears that some parents believe their most important priority is to train their teenagers how to be successful in school. They discipline their teenagers when it comes to homework and reward them when they achieve academically. They are often very engaged with them at school activities. These are commendable things for a parent to do, but should they be a number one priority?

Other parents push their teenagers to excel at sports. They buy the best of equipment for them. They coach them on the development of skills, and they work to make sure their teens are on the best teams. Some parents have even moved from one school district to another to give their child the best chance to succeed. Sports are certainly important. I have enjoyed participating in several sports throughout my own life. But is it worthy of first place?

Still other parents believe that the development of innate abilities in art, dance, or music should be a priority. Here again, they provide the necessary tools, spend the money to provide the best lessons, and encourage their children to be the best in their field. The arts are certainly important and we might well applaud those who allow their teenagers to excel in these areas of giftedness. But number one?

I know you may be wondering, *should parents encourage teenagers to excel in academics, sports, business, art, and so forth?* Parents should by all means encourage them to fulfill their God-given potential in any and every area for which He has created them. But that's the point! Parents and church leaders must nurture them to see any and every area of their lives as a platform for their kingdom service. They should be encouraged to excel precisely because their lives will have kingdom impact.

I can't leave this point yet. It would be too easy at this point to nod our head and whisper a quiet "amen," suggesting that we agree with establishing a kingdom priority. But let me ask a few more questions.

- Do the words and deeds of parents under your leadership communicate to their children that this kingdom focus is their number one priority?
- Do your teenagers know their parents want them to excel in areas of spiritual growth?

- Do parents under your leadership participate with their kids in Bible study and church activities with the same level of zeal they exhibit at sporting activities or school events?
- Are parents as concerned about their children's commitment to the memorization of Scripture as to their memorization of the multiplication tables?

In Ephesians 2:10 we read: *"For we are His creation—created in Christ Jesus for good works, which God prepared ahead of time so that we should walk in them."* Do you believe that each child is God's creation? If each child has a personal relationship with Christ, he or she is also a new creation in Him. Thus, they belong to Him by creation and by new birth.

But here's part of the equation you may have overlooked. God prepared good works beforehand that we might walk in them. Parents' kingdom goal should be to help each child discover God's preplanned good works and some practical ways to walk in them. Parents' number one priority should be to ensure that their children have a kingdom relationship and a kingdom purpose.

The Big Picture

Our goal in this book is to assist the church and the home to be partners in helping parents shape their teenagers to be kingdom agents. This is not simply a book about parenting, nor is it a book designed to tell you how to keep your teenagers in church. Truth be known, we have too many teenagers who have remained in church but:
- they still do not have a kingdom relationship;
- they do not have kingdom focus in their lives;
- they are not using their gifts for kingdom advancement;
- they do not know how to articulate and defend their faith;
- they are not looking at their career choice with the over-arching aim of using it to advance the kingdom of God.

The authors are not suggesting that every kingdom child should become what is frequently called a "career" or "vocational" missionary. That terminology may itself be somewhat confusing. We believe that every teenager should be raised with the conviction that they are called to be on mission regardless of their career track.

Once again, the word *career* might be misleading. The Bible doesn't speak about careers, but it does speak about mission. When we understand that we have been redeemed for the very purpose of joining God in His redemptive plan of providing every tribe, nation, and people group with the opportunity to respond to Him as their rightful King, it will transform every day into one of kingdom adventure. With this kingdom perspective, our parents and our teenagers will understand that the primary goal in life is to use their gifts, talents, resources, and setting in life as a platform for kingdom advancement.

While the kingdom needs what is conventionally termed "vocational missionaries," it also needs:

- athletes who see sports as a platform for kingdom advancement;
- artists and film producers who will use their creativity to advance God's kingdom—yes, right in Hollywood;
- doctors who see the hospital or clinic as a kingdom platform;
- teachers who will teach in public schools with a salt and light that creates hunger and thirst for their kingdom perspective;
- lawyers seeking an opportunity to advance God's kingdom in a field too often known only for its legal opportunists;
- nurses who see their care for their patients in a broader kingdom context;
- politicians who are willing to live out kingdom truths;
- pastors and staff members who are more concerned about advancing God's kingdom than building their own churches;
- factory workers who know that they have been given the opportunity to minister daily to many who have lost hope;
- secretaries who see the nobility of their task in terms of the King in whose duty they truly serve;
- craftsmen who understand the source of their giftedness and celebrate it with quality;
- business leaders who understand that kingdom ethics require fair business practices.

We invite you to add to the list as you help parents and teenagers discover their giftedness. Kingdom focus is that one component that will enable you to work with parents to challenge their teenagers to seek excellence in every area of activity. All too often, our desire to achieve excellence can be selfishly motivated and thus create a sense of arrogance. When the parent encourages the child to seek excellence based on the kingdom of God, a new perspective is gained.

Kingdom focus will help parents guide teenagers in decisions that will impact their lives—decisions concerning premarital sex, drugs, and drinking. Can we, as parents, present a compelling case for abstinence? We can if we connect it with our child's relationship to the King who is their Creator.

We live a different lifestyle because we belong to a King who is holy, and we would never want to do anything that would dishonor His name. We remain pure because we desire to be the most effective instrument possible in the hands of the King. We remain pure because we know that the Father loves us and desires only the best for us.

What Now?

As you read, you will no doubt find yourself saying, "I wish I had known this earlier." You may wonder where this book was when you needed it most. What do you do if you have already blown it in some of the issues that we will talk about in this book? You may find yourself wondering what you should do now. Good question.

Come clean! Tell your parents and teenagers what God has been teaching you and apologize for blowing it. Admit that you will probably blow it again, but confess that you are asking the Father to help you develop kingdom-focused parents and teenagers. Admit that this is a new journey for you and that you will have to grow along with your parents and youth.

Let me warn you that your parents and teenagers may not readily respond to this new-found commitment and zeal to put the kingdom first. Be patient and be willing to laugh at your own mistakes. Time and love will ultimately win out as kingdom focus begins to make a difference in your church.

Kingdom focus is not easy for any of us to choose. After all, the kingdoms of this world are appealing! Your teenagers want to be accepted as popular. They want to fit in. They want to succeed. You can help parents and teenagers understand that God created them with a desire for community. You can remind them that the desire to have friends is important, but it is equally important to have the right kind of friends.

You can teach parents and their youth the difference between temporal and eternal values in the din of everyday activity. These lessons will probably last longer than those learned at family devotions.

As a staff partner, you have the unique and holy privilege of preparing your parents and teenagers to become kingdom agents. This book is designed with this singular focus in mind. There is nothing you will do that will have more lasting significance than this task. What profit would there be if we raised our teenagers with the skills and personality to rule a business enterprise but in return they pay with the loss of kingdom focus? Is it worth the risk?

I know of two things for certain. I want to see my children in heaven, and I want to be standing in the front row when the King says to them, "Well done good and faithful kingdom agent, enter now into the kingdom."

It may be a slight paraphrase, but it is a good one.

CHAPTER TWO

Scripture and Kingdom Parenting

Ken Hemphill

MANY CHRISTIAN LEADERS AND PARENTS are frustrated when it comes to instilling in their teenagers the level of kingdom commitment they have. Now I am talking about good leaders and parents, folks who love their kids and have worked to employ good ministry and parenting techniques. Yet good techniques may not produce the level of kingdom commitment that these adults desire.

In this chapter we are going to look to the Bible for principles and models, good and bad, of people who attempted to pass on kingdom priorities. This should be an obvious place to start. After all, we need to consult with the One who wrote the Book on instilling kingdom focus. When we read the pages of the New Testament, it doesn't take long to see that Jesus shared His Father's passion for the kingdom. We can see it in His life and His teaching. Let's learn from the best.

The Deuteronomy 6 Model

> *"Listen, Israel: The LORD our God, the LORD is One. Love the LORD your God with all your heart, with all your soul, and with all your strength. These words that I am giving you today are to be in your heart. Repeat them to your children. Talk about them when you sit in your house and when you walk along the road, when you lie down and when you get up. Bind them as a sign on your hand and let them be a symbol on your forehead. Write them on the doorposts of your house and on your gates"* (Deut. 6:4-8).

You may recognize the words of this text. They make up the core statement of Israel's faith and are known in Judaism as "the Shema," and they will serve as the foundation for many of the truths shared in this book. The word *shema* is the transliteration of the first Hebrew word in verse 4, which can be translated *listen* or *hear*. We shouldn't overlook the impact of the simple word *hear*. It suggests that the heart of biblical religion, and therefore kingdom living, is the conviction that God has spoken. As a result, we must conform our beliefs and behaviors to His revealed Word.

The central truth articulated in the Shema is the confession that God is One. This points to His uniqueness and supremacy. It underlines the conviction that God is not one member of a pantheon of gods, but He is uniquely God. This is not a popular conviction to hold in our day. The pluralistic and politically correct climate today finds this a narrow and somewhat bigoted view. Yet this conviction is central to everything the Bible says; therefore, it is the fundamental axiom on which this book is based.

If one agrees that God alone is God, then He also is sovereign and supreme. That means the most important thing we, His creatures, can do is love and serve Him. We owe Him our affection, worship, and absolute allegiance. Notice this very emphasis in verse 5. We are to love God with our heart, soul, and strength. This expression is frequently repeated in Deuteronomy (4:29; 10:12; 11:13; 13:3, 26:16: 30:2,6). Our obedience and service do not come from legalistic fear, but from a relationship based on God's unfailing and redemptive love.

In Hebrew thinking, the "heart" referred to the locus of the intellect and the will, as well as the seat of a wide range of emotions. For example Zechariah 8:17 indicates one thinks with the heart: *"Let none of you think evil in your heart against your neighbor..."* (NKJV). The term "soul" is difficult to define, but it seems to refer to the source of life and vitality in a person.

Thus, when used together, heart and soul suggest that we must love God with our whole being—our unreserved devotion. This demand for commitment is given further weight by the addition of "strength." This refers not so much to physical strength as to intensity. God desires not merely that "we possess a faith but that our faith should possess us."[1]

Lest you think this is an Old Testament reference with little value for the New Testament believer, you should note that Jesus used this statement to summarize the whole duty of man. When one of the scribes asked Jesus about the most important commandment, He responded:

"'This is the most important,' Jesus answered; 'Listen, Israel! The Lord our God, the Lord is One. Love the Lord your God with all your heart, with all your soul, with all your mind, and with all your strength'" (Mark. 12:29-30).

God's truths are to be placed into the hearts of His people rather than being codified on stone tablets. We have had some interesting debates lately about having the Ten Commandments displayed in public places, such as courthouses. God is much more concerned that His commandments be written in the hearts of His people and displayed in their character than their presence in any physical building. To have God's law written on our hearts indicates our wholehearted desire to obey God's Word and to allow that obedience to be reflected in our character. This is the essence of kingdom behavior.

Kingdom parents, however, are not content with personal obedience alone. Their desire is to pass along this kingdom heritage to their children. The Hebrew language uses a word that is often used to describe the sharpening of a knife on a whetstone.[1] Parents are responsible for "honing" their teenagers in such a way that those teenagers can be effective kingdom agents.

I know this Deuteronomy model sounds radically different from the popular model of parenting that says we should give our teenagers all the options in an atmosphere of neutrality and let them decide for themselves the direction and purpose of their lives. This is truly not an option for the kingdom-focused parent.

We must *"train up a child in the way he [or she] should go"* (Prov. 22:6, KJV). Trust me, there is no such thing as a neutral environment. The world will exert constant and intense pressure on your teenagers to follow the natural instincts of the flesh and to live for their own gratification. Parents and leaders cannot decide for teenagers, but they can provide the atmosphere and training that will help them to see the value of kingdom living.

This passage is prescriptive when it comes to accomplishing kingdom-focused parenting, and it serves as a foundational reference point for this book. Parents should seize every opportunity to engage in spiritual training. Notice that it is comprehensive in scope: "when you lie down and when you get up." Further, it involves both formal and informal sessions: "when you sit in your house and when you walk along the road." Kingdom parents will strive to help their teenagers interpret every facet of life in terms of its kingdom impact.

The command to bind the law on hand and forehead and to write it on the doorposts and gates was taken literally in some expressions of Judaism. The origin for the phylacteries and *mezuzah* is to be found in this passage, but the intent of this passage is too significant to be satisfied by physical adornments to the body or house. Remember we have already seen that God desires that this law be written on the heart. God wants His people to be constantly aware of His moral standards and to use them as the guidelines for their every action and activity.

If we follow this God-given model for kingdom parenting, we will be able to ensure that kingdom priority is passed from generation to generation.

Biblical Examples of Kingdom Parenting

The Bible provides us numerous examples—both good and bad—for helping us to learn to be effective kingdom parents. Before we look at several practical suggestions, let's take a look at several intriguing examples.

ABRAHAM AND ISAAC

You may recall that Abraham's faith pilgrimage centered on God's promise to make Him a mighty nation so that he and his descendants would bless the nations (Gen. 12:1-3). Remember, blessing is given to be conveyed, not consumed. Isaac was born to Abraham in his old age. In Genesis 22, God commands Abraham to take Isaac to the land of Moriah and offer him as a burnt offering. Abraham, by this juncture in his faith pilgrimage, knows with absolute certainty that God is fully trustworthy.[2]

Without pause, Abraham set out for Mount Moriah with his son Isaac. On the way to worship, Isaac asked his father a penetrating question:

"The fire and the wood are here, but where is the lamb for the burnt offering?" (v. 7). Listen to the reply of his father: *"God Himself will provide the lamb for the burnt offering, my son"* (v. 8).

Wow! What confidence! What a lesson!

You may recall the rest of the story. At the last moment, God stopped

26

Abraham and showed him a lamb that had already been provided. Abraham declared that now he knew that God is *Jehovah Jireh*—the Lord who provides. Abraham provided a faith lesson for us on the way.

It is fascinating that years later Isaac dug again the wells that his father had originally dug (Gen. 26:18-25). This may seem insignificant in our day when our water comes from the city reservoir; but in the days of Abraham, the digging of wells and the provision of water was critical. When we follow the life of Isaac, we can detect the influence of his father.

DAVID AND SOLOMON

The great King David passionately desired to build the temple where God's name would dwell. God informed him that he would not be allowed to build the temple, but He assured David that his son would be allowed to take on the project. David devoted the remainder of his time as king to providing the resources that would enable his son to build the temple. In fact, in 2 Samuel 7, David broke forth into praise for the greatness of God.

Solomon did indeed complete the temple that would become the centerpiece of Israel's worship. When Solomon dedicated the temple, his prayer and praise reflected not only the sentiment of his father, but even his language. No doubt David's passion had been transferred to his son.

> "It was in the desire of my father David to build a temple for the name of the LORD God of Israel...The LORD has fulfilled what He promised. I have taken the place of my father David, and I sit on the throne of Israel, as the LORD promised. I have built the temple for the name of the LORD God of Israel" (1 Kings 8:17,20).

ELKANAH, HANNAH, ELI, AND SAMUEL

While 1 Samuel begins with a reference to Elkanah, the primary focus is on his son Samuel and his wife Hannah. The tragedy of the story is that Hannah was barren. Barrenness is a difficult burden in our day, but it was often seen as a reproach in Hannah's day.

Elkanah and his family went to Shiloh, an important center for worship, on a regular basis. It was on these occasions that Hannah would pour out her heart to God. She was praying for a son, but not just to cure her barrenness. She vowed to give him to the Lord for His service (1 Sam. 1:11). Eli, the priest, noticed the fervency of her prayer, but he mistook it for drunkenness since her lips were moving but he heard no words. When Hannah explained her anguish, he sent her away in peace and with the assurance that God had heard her prayers.

In due time, Samuel was born. After he was weaned (a period that may have been as long as three years), Hannah took him to Shiloh and left him with Eli so that he might serve the Lord all his days.

Woven into this touching story of the birth of Samuel is the tragic dissolution of the family of Eli. *"Eli's sons were wicked men; they had no regard for the LORD"* (1 Sam. 2:12). That is a sad epithet for the house or life of any person!

We have quite a contrast between the son of Elkanah and Hannah and the sons of Eli. While Eli's sons were condemned, the boy Samuel grew up in the presence of the Lord (2:21). Eli's sons would not listen to their father, but the boy Samuel grew in stature and in favor with the Lord and with men (2:25b-26).

Do you wonder why this priest failed to pass on his passion for the things of God to his sons while Elkanah and Hannah succeeded? The key is found in 2:29: *"...You have honored your sons more than Me..."* Eli had made the tragic mistake of putting his children before his commitment to the Lord. Elkanah and Hannah on the other hand had given their child to the Lord.

Samuel grew up to be one of the mighty men of God. He was chosen to anoint the first two kings of Israel. Growing up in Shiloh, Samuel would have known of his father's passion for worship as he brought his family regularly to offer sacrifice. He must have been greatly influenced by the knowledge that his mother had first offered him to the Lord and that his father had affirmed that decision. When I read this story, I sometimes wonder if God was giving Eli a second chance with Samuel. Eli had failed with his own sons, but God allowed him to nurture Samuel in the things of faith.

One of the most important things parents can do for their teenagers is to participate with them in worship and release them to the Lord. When we release them to the Lord, they will know of our kingdom focus.

Think back to the story I told in the last chapter about the mother I met at the conference center. This mother literally could not bear the thought of her daughter leaving her for the mission field. She was afraid to give her child completely to the plan and purpose of God. I gently reminded her that the only way she truly could keep her daughter was to give her to the Lord. The day may come when you or the parents with whom you work face a similar challenge.

Not every teenager will be called to a foreign mission field, but each one is redeemed for service. God saved him or her for His plan and purpose, and parents must recognize the greatest joy comes in seeing their children accomplish God's calling for their lives. Youth leaders can encourage parents to give their children to the Lord early and often, and to let their teenagers know that they have made this commitment. The result will be a greater degree of kingdom focus for both the parents and their children.

DANIEL, HANANIAH, MISHAEL, AND AZARIAH

The nation of Israel had been taken into Babylonian captivity. Nebuchadnezzar, the king of Babylon, ordered his chief court official to choose some of the Israelite youth to bring into his court for training. His criteria for selection were stiff—"*Young men without any physical defect, good-looking, suitable for instruction in all wisdom, knowledgeable, perceptive, and capable of serving in the king's palace*" (Dan. 1:4).

These young men were to be taught Chaldean language and literature, and they were to be fed from the royal table (1:4-5). It may not come as a surprise that some of the Chaldean food would not meet the standards of Jewish culture, but you may not have thought that the Chaldean literature also would run contrary to the worldview of these Jewish youth who had been taught to worship God alone.

These young Jews dared to defy the king by refusing to break the kosher guidelines and eat his food. While Daniel and his friends were quite respectful in every regard, it is apparent that these youth had grown to share the conviction of their parents. They had been nurtured according to the Deuteronomy 6 model. When they were separated from their parents, they still stood as young men of conviction.

I am even more impressed that when confronted with a pagan worldview, they retained their own convictions. Will your teenagers be able to stand when confronted by the secular worldview they will be taught in school? If they are well-trained at home by the consistent teaching and modeling of parents, they will not only stand, they will be able to thrive.

When these young men were tested by the pagan king, they passed with flying colors. *"In every matter of wisdom and understanding that the king consulted them about, he found them 10 times better than all the diviner-priests and mediums in his entire kingdom"* (1:20). Why? *"God gave these young men knowledge and understanding in every kind of literature and wisdom"* (1:17). If we are going to advance the kingdom, we need to develop teenagers who can stand and thrive.

Lois, Eunice, and Timothy

Paul was preparing to pass the torch to young Timothy, his protégé. The two letters that go by his name have led many to suggest that Timothy felt a bit intimidated by the thought of filling those large shoes. In the second letter to Timothy, Paul encouraged him by reference to his "sincere faith" which had first lived in his grandmother Lois and then in his mother Eunice (2 Tim. 1:5). This characteristic of unalloyed faith had been transmitted from generation to generation to generation.

According to Acts 16:1-3, Timothy's father was Greek and his mother Eunice was a "believing Jewish woman." The omission of any mention of Timothy's father in 2 Timothy probably indicates he was not a believer. We are not told enough to know how or when these two women were converted to Christianity, but it is apparent that their piety and faith had greatly influenced Timothy. Based on this awareness of Timothy's noble heritage, Paul exhorted him to keep the gift of God in him ablaze. He then notes: *"For God has not given us a spirit of fearfulness, but one of power, love, and sound judgment"* (1:7).

This passage should be a great encouragement to any parent who finds himself or herself as the only believing parent. They still can pass on a great, spiritual heritage to their teenagers.

ENDNOTES

1. Doug McIntosh, *Deuteronomy* in Holman Old Testament Commentary (Nashville: Broadman and Holman, 2002), 86.

2. If you want to read more about how God revealed His character to Abraham to build his faith, we recommend *The Names of God* by Ken Hemphill. (Nashville: Broadman and Holman, 2001). You will find chapter 6 particularly helpful.

CHAPTER THREE

Who Teenagers Think God Is

Rick Morton

TO CONSIDER THE STATE OF FAITH among Southern Baptist teenagers, we must begin by understanding the true underpinnings of their faith. On the surface, this task seems simple enough. If we can know what teenagers believe and the degree to which they are committed to their beliefs, we can evaluate our efforts as families and churches in helping them achieve a mature faith in Christ. This understanding of the faith status of teenagers within the Southern Baptist Convention (SBC) also makes it possible to predict correct courses of action for ministry.

31

Any study of SBC teenagers must be grounded in the core beliefs embraced by Southern Baptists. Only then can we really understand what we observe about their behavior or determine ways to encourage their growth in Christ. In essence, we must answer an important question to guide our work: What issue or factor is most central to the belief and practice of Southern Baptist teenagers?

God: The Beginning Point for Understanding Faith

To answer this important question, I would suggest that we must begin by considering what our teenagers believe about God. After all, God is the center of our faith. He is the Creator and Source of all that we know or can imagine. He is the object of our worship. Faith, values, and the resulting actions of people flow from what they believe about God.

Once we construct a picture of what teenagers know, understand, and are committed to about God, we are in a position to make sense of many other observations about their attitudes and behaviors. We must understand the picture of God they own and use to operate on a daily basis. Until we are able to do that, we are left to guess about how to minister to them, without the ability to affect the core convictions that underlie their thoughts and motivate their actions.

Teenagers Believe in God

The data from the National Study of Youth and Religion show some encouraging news about Southern Baptist teenagers with regard to their belief in God. As can be seen in Table 1, the 96 percent of Southern Baptist teenagers who profess belief in God represent the second highest rate of belief in God for any group or denomination in the study. While not altogether surprising, it is comforting to know that virtually every Southern Baptist teenager holds a professed belief in the existence of God.

The practical significance of this finding is somewhat questionable in light of the apparent state of faith and practice in the larger American adolescent culture. To a lesser extent, data from the study indicate that most other American teens share a commitment to a belief in the existence of God regardless of their religious affiliation. The Judeo-Christian notion of God which has been present since the founding of the country still exists on some level in this rising generation.

Properly, we must question the depth and quality of this professed belief in God among American teenagers because their lives offer little evidence that they operate daily from a God-centered worldview. While large numbers of American teenagers profess belief in God, their actions often reflect belief in themselves or in the norms of their culture as the standard by which they live.

TABLE 1. BELIEFS ABOUT GOD AND ROLE OF FAITH (PERCENTAGES)

	Believe in God	Experienced a Definite Answer to Prayer or Specific Guidance from God	Made a Personal Commitment to Live Your Life for God	Believe in Judgment Day	Faith Is Very or Extremely Important in Shaping How They Live Life Daily
Southern Baptist Convention	96	66	80	88	72
Conservative Protestant	94	65	79	88	67
Mainline Protestant	86	53	60	63	50
Black Protestant	97	61	74	91	73

	Believe in God	Experienced a Definite Answer to Prayer or Specific Guidance from God	Made a Personal Commitment to Live Your Life for God	Believe in Judgment Day	Faith Is Very or Extremely Important in Shaping How They Live Life Daily
All Protestants	93	61	73	83	66
Catholic	85	42	41	67	41
Unaffiliated	62	24	27	49	23
All Teenagers	84	50	55	71	51

Source: National Study of Youth and Religion, 2002-3.

Teenagers Plan to Live for God

There are other seemingly positive observations in the NSYR's data regarding our teenagers' perception of God. Eighty percent of Southern Baptist teenagers reported having "made a personal commitment to live [their life] for God." This means that they not only admitted to believing in God, but readily declared what they described as a personal commitment to live for Him.

We must not stretch too far in interpreting the nature of this commitment. The statistics do not necessarily support the notion that the overwhelming majority of SBC teenagers have made a saving commitment of their lives to Christ. The questions asked in this research do not reveal whether these teenagers have experienced Christian conversion.

Instead, the data point to a more troubling sign that SBC teenagers are dedicated to the less specific goal of living their lives for God. Many of the teenagers who believe in God and are committed to living their lives for Him could believe their active obedience will earn their salvation. From this data, we cannot be certain what teenagers mean by this commitment. Interpretation of other data from the study may shed some light on the nature of the commitment they profess.

God's Sovereignty

SBC teenagers seem to accept some notion of God's right to authority over them. This is made clear by their acknowledgment of God's divine right to judge the lives of all people. In fact, 88 percent of Southern Baptist teenagers claim belief in the existence of a judgment day. At least in matters of eternal judgment, SBC teenagers report a high regard for God's ultimate authority over humanity.

This finding cannot be overlooked in determining the overall perception of God held by SBC teenagers. In large numbers they accept God's rule over them. It follows that they would be interested in shaping their lives to please God since they believe He will judge them.

God's Influence for Living

Most teenagers appear to have made the connection between belief and behavior. Seventy-two percent of SBC teenagers report that their faith in God is "very or extremely important to shaping how they live daily life." Most SBC teenagers seem to make a natural connection between God, His nature, His divine judgment of creation, and the way they live each day. It is interesting to note the small, but significant, number of teenagers who have apparently disassociated their belief in God and beliefs about God from their daily living.

More than one-quarter of the SBC teenagers who professed a belief in God report having no meaningful connection between their belief in God and how they choose to live each day. Table 1 describes teenagers who have experienced answered prayer or guidance from God. It further illuminates this disconnect. Approximately one-third of the Southern Baptist teenagers who profess to believe in God said that they have never experienced an answer to prayer or specific guidance from God. While the large majority of SBC students seem to have a faith that reflects intimacy with God through answered prayer and guidance for life, the numbers of teenagers for whom belief in God is apparently an empty exercise is alarming.

Beliefs about God's Nature

Much of the disconnect between beliefs in and about God and the influence of those beliefs upon life may relate to how teenagers view the nature of God. In Table 2, we see that more than three-fourths of Southern Baptist teenagers report a belief that God is a personal being who is involved in the lives of people. Relatively few (14 percent) hold to a purely deistic view of God that acknowledges God's creative work but denies His continued work in His creation. Even fewer (8 percent), hold to the transcendental view that God is an impersonal, cosmic life force much like the concept of God set forth in Hinduism and many New Age religions.

The percentage of SBC teenagers who hold to an orthodox view of God's personal, involved role in this world is a very positive sign. But again, the significant size of the groups holding to the minority view is noteworthy. We can infer that fully one-fifth of SBC teenagers have a view of God's nature that is completely inconsistent with God's revelation about Himself in the Bible.

TABLE 2. VIEWS OF GOD (PERCENTAGES)

	Definitely Believe in the Possibility of Divine Miracles from God	God Is a Personal Being Involved in the Lives of People Today	God Created the World, But Is Not Involved in the World Now	God Is Not Personal, But Something Like a Cosmic Force	Feel Very or Extremely Close to God
Southern Baptist Convention	74	76	14	8	49
Conservative Protestant	77	77	10	8	48
Mainline Protestant	59	69	13	13	40
Black Protestant	76	74	13	7	49
All Protestants	71	74	13	9	47
Catholic	55	64	17	14	31
Unaffiliated	35	41	20	35	18
All Teenagers	61	65	13	14	36

Source: National Study of Youth and Religion, 2002-3.

SBC teenagers also believe in a powerful God who is capable of superseding the limits of His creation. Almost three-quarters (74 percent) of them profess to believe in the possibility of miracles from God. Evidently, most SBC teenagers recognize the ever-present power of God to act in and among His creation without limitation.

It is also noteworthy to recognize the similarity in the percentage of teenagers who see God as involved in people's lives and those who believe in God's power for miracles. It appears that most SBC teenagers have made the connection between God's power over creation and His ongoing involvement in creation. This positive finding presents an opportunity to help teenagers connect their belief in God's power and activity with the personal nature of a relationship to Christ.

Closeness with God

Perhaps the most disturbing finding by the NSYR involves the data regarding closeness to God. Just less than half (49 percent) of SBC students reported being "very or extremely" close to God. While we recognize that feelings are subjective, the idea that most SBC teenagers have healthy, orthodox beliefs about God without a sense of intimacy with Him is alarming. After all, adolescents are emotional beings. In most cases, their ability to feel and experience emotion is more adult-like than their ability to think critically and employ logical reasoning.

Adolescents move from concrete experience to the ability to comprehend and embrace abstract truth. If teenagers are missing experiences that help them connect to God, we may be missing an opportunity to help teenagers develop a holistic faith built on both feeling and reason.

Interpreting SBC Teenagers' Beliefs about God

These research observations lead to some general conclusions about today's SBC teenagers and their perceptions of God. On the whole, the news is good. The majority of Southern Baptist teenagers seem to be fairly orthodox in their beliefs about God, His person, and His activity. Comparing the SBC data to the available data from other denominations and groups underscores the relatively positive condition of SBC teenagers. Furthermore, a majority of these teenagers appear to be translating their beliefs into appropriate convictions and actions.

Unfortunately, a significant minority of SBC teenagers profess fairly traditional, biblical beliefs about God but have other convictions and values that stand in contrast to their stated beliefs. For these teenagers, the data present a less than favorable picture. Their fundamental beliefs about God appear to be drawn from sources outside of biblical Christianity. As many as one-fourth of SBC teenagers have views of God that are profoundly inconsistent with who God has revealed Himself to be. We must be concerned that a significant number of teenagers within the influence of our families and churches are not connecting with some of the most important truths we want to pass to them.

Teenagers Acting as "Functional Deists"

While the majority of SBC teenagers reject a deistic or transcendental view of God, many actually may be embracing a form of functional deism.[1] These teenagers can answer questions about the nature of God that point to His continued activity in the lives of people. At the same time, their lifestyles suggest that they ignore the work of God in their daily affairs. While most of the SBC teenagers said they believe God is a personal being who is involved in people's lives, many do not appear convinced of this to the point that they are willing to live that way.

Consider some of the self-reported behaviors and attitudes of SBC teenagers found in Table 3. Forty-one percent have come to believe that morals are relative. But as presented earlier, a significant portion also claim to believe in a God who is personal and who is very or extremely important to shaping how they live. Putting these observations together, we must conclude that this significant segment of SBC teenagers have an intellectual commitment to the existence of God, but a functional disregard for His active role in defining morality or shaping their response to it.

The Spiritual Disciplines

Another inconsistency between the teenagers' view of God and their actions can be found in their lack of practice in spiritual disciplines such as Bible reading (39 percent) or fasting and self-denial (19 percent). While a fairly large number of SBC teenagers report praying multiple times a week (67 percent), the small number of SBC teenagers' involvement in disciplines such as personal Bible reading and fasting could indicate a lack of intimacy on their part in relating to God. Again, while they would not consciously support an explanation of God as an uninvolved, passive Creator, their lack of activity to foster intimacy with God combined with their lack of feeling close to God would indicate they are operating with an unbiblical and flawed understanding of the God they acknowledge.

TABLE 3. SELECTED BELIEFS AND BEHAVIORS (PERCENTAGES)

	Agree That Morals Are Relative	Read the Bible Alone Once a Week or More	Fasted or Denied Self Something as a Spiritual Discipline in Last Year
Southern Baptist Convention	41	39	19
Conservative Protestant	37	37	22
Mainline Protestant	50	20	21
Black Protestant	36	36	20
All Protestants	41	32	21
Catholic	50	13	29
Unaffiliated	66	13	6
All Teenagers	45	26	24

Source: National Study of Youth and Religion, 2002-3.

Teenagers Acting as Faith Consumers

Consumerism and the related issues of choice and consumption also seem to be important factors in what teenagers believe about God. Issues of economy and consumerism are overwhelmingly significant social factors in the environment of the American teenager. Today's adolescents are one of the most targeted demographic segments in the American economy—and with good reason. In 2003, American teenagers spent a total of $175 billion. That comes to an average of $103 per teenager each week, and most of that money is disposable income.[2] Businesses have learned that teenagers represent a significant potential revenue stream. From the constant marketing attention afforded teenagers and the corresponding emphasis upon their power to choose, many teenagers have embraced a mistaken notion of self-importance and self-determination.

This exalted view of self tends to reinforce functional deism. Convinced by culture that they have both ultimate power and the sovereign right to make decisions, even Christian teenagers experience daily life on their own without real regard for God's presence. They seem comfortable acting as if God is an uninvolved, dispassionate observer of their lives instead of the ever-present, personal, and involved Creator of the Bible.

Teenagers also can be comfortable mixing the Christian faith and other religions. They consider a smorgasbord of beliefs and axioms from which they shop for elements to form a personal faith system. What results is a fluid, personal theology based upon the desires of the young person instead of an objective theology that flows from the unchanging person and character of God.

The abundance of marketing pitches crafted for teenagers seems to have led to a spirit of entitlement that overemphasizes their perceived right to self-comfort and self-gratification. American teens can choose from an abundance of options in almost every area of life. It is easy to see how even Christian teenagers can be lulled into believing important things in life derive importance because the individual chooses to make them so.

Instead of relying on God to set boundaries and priorities, many Christian teenagers have become comfortable choosing their own limits and constraints. They feel little or no tension living inconsistently with their professed beliefs. They choose those things they believe and those things they wish to do with little or no objectivity (like biblical standards) in the evaluation of their choices.

Many consumer-driven teenagers are approaching God with the same man-centered view of their faith that they see in the adult world. Essentially, they are approaching God and the church asking a simple question: "What's in it for me?" They struggle with the concept of worship because they mistakenly seek to be entertained by an experience. They struggle with stewardship because they are looking for a return on their spending. They serve to receive a good feeling.

Impact of Media

Many Christian teenagers seem prone to act in ways that are inconsistent with their intellectual convictions. One interesting hypothesis for this phenomenon involves the influence of media on postmodern teenagers. Contemporary media outlets use powerful visual and auditory tools to touch individuals on the emotional level. Adolescents who have yet to perfect the rational thinking ability of an adult are more easily influenced by the powerful emotional presentations from media outlets. In this regard they are unlike adults who have learned to think more critically and have more life experience through which to filter the content. Combining the rising volume of media consumption and the declining moral content in the media they are consuming, it is easy to see how media can shape the worldviews of our teenagers.

Another interesting consideration regarding the role of media is how teenagers see God in that media. The media industry is in the business of capturing attention in order to influence spending. Spiritual things are interesting to teenagers, so Hollywood has no apprehension about addressing matters of spirituality, even the Bible, in ways that are unbiblical and theologically unsound. Sadly, many teenagers are using media representations of God and faith as a viable source of information as they shape their theological belief systems.

Conclusion

Many of the implications of this data and other observations about what teenagers believe about God are troubling. There can be no doubt that there is much work to be done, but perhaps the first step toward action is understanding. By understanding the situation, we are able to begin an objective assessment of where our teenagers are and how effective parents and leaders have been in making an impact on them.

Most of all, we must realize that the God we want our teenagers to know is active in reaching out to them. We want to help teenagers discover who God is and how forming a personal relationship with Him always has been His agenda for their lives. As adults, we must seek to know God more fully and understand Him better through the revelation of His Word.

Our intimacy with God and our reflection of His character provide our best opportunities for making an impact on the next generation.

ENDNOTES

1. The author was first introduced to the term *functional deist* by Dr. Christian Smith, the principle researcher for the National Study of Youth and Religion. The term was presented in a discussion of the implications of the NSYR research upon which much of this book is based.

2. Teenage Research Unlimited, "Teens Spent $175 Billion in 2003." Online at *http://www.teenresearch.com/PRview.cfm?edit_id=168*, cited 15 September 2004.

CHAPTER FOUR

Introducing Teenagers to God

Tom Wilks

MATT WAS FRUSTRATED. He had taken a week off to evaluate the youth ministry he had been leading for the past year and a half. As he looked at the statistical information, he felt that he had been successful. Every time there was a fellowship, nearly every chair was taken. Summer camp had maxed out both summers he had been at Salem Church. Sunday morning Bible study was growing steadily. He felt that he had strong support from parents, youth workers, the pastor, and the church staff. Still, he was frustrated. It seemed as if the spiritual dimension of the youth group was very shallow. Even though teenagers were making professions of faith and being baptized, there seemed to be little understanding of the Christian faith or of the biblical revelation.

As Matt thought about the youth group, he remembered a comment he had read. The "church is one mile long, but only one inch deep."[1]

Could the source of his frustration be active, religious kids who are not growing spiritually?

A Conventional Faith

American stereotypes define teenagers as stormy and rebellious. Entertainment depicts adolescents as alone, disillusioned, irreverent, and rebellious. The National Study of Youth and Religion offers a different view of youth. The findings showed that a vast majority of American teens are very conventional in their religious identity and practice.[2]

For example, when American teenagers talk about the origins of their religious identity, interests, and beliefs, the vast majority said they simply believe what they were raised to believe. They are simply following in their family's religious footsteps (120). While some teens are disgruntled with the congregation where their parents worship, the majority seems to be happy attending religious services at the same congregation and with the same frequency as their parents (121).

While a majority of American teenagers follow the faith of their family, there is a minority that holds differing positions. They no longer follow the faith of their parents. Most of these teenagers do not make an issue of their divergent views with their parents (122).

It is also interesting to note that there is little conflict between teenagers and family members over religious matters. Few adolescents in the United States talk with friends about religious matters, and even fewer get into arguments when they do discuss religion. Thus, religion is not a contested or conflictive part in the lives of most teenagers in today's adolescent culture (123-124).

In reality, a large majority of teenagers see religion as a positive force in society and in the life of an individual. Generally, adolescents believe that religion helps provide people with strong moral foundations. As a result, teenagers see religion as positive because it "gives people morals" and provides "something to believe in." Therefore, most of those interviewed in the NSYR value and appreciate religion because it helps accomplish those things (125-127).

It should be pointed out that most of the nonreligious teenagers interviewed in the study expressed open and positive views concerning religion. The vast majority of teenagers in the United States express little if any rebellion against, aggravation with, or hostility toward religion, including "organized religion." At the very worse, the vast majority of American teenagers see religion in a benignly positive light (127).

A few of the teenagers who were interviewed in the study had explored or were in the process of exploring religions other than the one in which they had been raised. Many of those who were doing so were not seriously considering changing faiths. They were simply on a quest to "just learn more" (128).

The Importance of Religion to the American Teenager

Teenagers tend to be religious, and they are generally positive about and conventional in living out religion. However, this does not mean that religion is among the most important concerns in the average adolescent's life.

When teenagers were asked directly how important religion was in their lives, some said that religion is not important at all or that it is only somewhat important. However, many teens did state that religion is very important to them. They indicated that religion serves as the basis for their fundamental knowledge of right and wrong (129-130).

A Background Issue for Many

As noted, religion does not seem to appear on most teenagers' open-ended lists of what matters most in their lives. The lives of many American adolescents are dominated by issues related to school and homework. Then there are sports, clubs, friends, television, movies, instant messaging, listening to music, and using other electronic media. With so many distractions, it is not hard to understand why many teenagers have not placed their relationship with God on the front burner of their lives.

In many ways, religion and faith issues are just another "piece" in the puzzles that represent adolescent existence. Religion is not an integral aspect of teens' structured lives, and it does not come up often as a relevant subject in their discussions outside of church. It is seldom part of a teenager's most significant social relationships. In a very real sense, religion has become rather compartmentalized. It simply resides in the background for most teenagers in the United States.

Inarticulate about Their Faith

While teenagers tend to be religious, the majority are very inarticulate about their faith, their religious beliefs and practices, and the meaning or place of those beliefs and practices in their lives. Researchers found very few teens from any religious background who could describe their religious beliefs well or explain how those beliefs connected to the rest of their lives (131). The interviewers got the impression that many of the teenagers had not been effectively educated in and provided opportunities to practice talking about their faith. Indeed, researchers working on the NSYR project came away with a very real sense that their interviewing process was the first time any of those teenagers had been asked to express their faith in a substantive way and to explain the impact it had on their everyday lives (133).

Don't Know Their Faith Traditions

Another observation from the NSYR is that many teens either do not know what their faith traditions say they are supposed to believe, or they do not understand it. In other cases, they may know what they are supposed to believe, but they simply do not choose to believe it. This raises the question of whether teens have made a personal decision against being interested in explaining and living out what they believe or whether their faith communities have failed to educate them on the importance of these issues.

Whichever may be true, the result is that most religious teenagers' perceptions of religion are vague (at best) and often contradict the actual teachings of their own religious tradition. While American adolescents may know a lot about popular music, television shows, sports personalities, and other media-related aspects of culture, they may not be very familiar with key historical figures of their faith, such as Moses and Jesus (134). In addition, they may have no clue as to why those historical figures can or should have any influence on their lives.

Unclear about Salvation

Since teenagers have difficulty explaining what they believe, it should not come as a surprise that the great majority seem unable to grasp the basics of salvation. For example, the sampling of responses taken from the NSYR included the following adolescent responses:

- *A 15 year-old boy from Mississippi.* If you do the right thing and don't do anything bad, I mean nothing really bad, you know you'll go to heaven. If you don't, then you're screwed (laughs), that's about it.
- *A 16 year-old girl from Pennsylvania.* Being a Christian means, um, don't do many sins, read the Bible, go to church, living godly, that's about it. It's basically not committing sin, basically.
- *A 13 year-old boy from Ohio.* God is just this big thing that's been there forever and controls everything, probably not personal, I don't know. (How did you come to that idea?) Ah, like I was just raised that way I guess, and I guess I believe it till I hear another theory that's more reasonable or something, like from science.
- *An 18 year-old girl from Maryland.* My beliefs are so wishy-washy, like I'll think something one minute, something else the next. I don't know what is most important, cause I don't really live by the Bible.
- *A 17 year-old girl from Illinois.* I guess I'm a Christian, but I'm one of those still trying to figure everything out. I believe there's a higher power, but that's about all I know for sure (136-137).

The majority of American teenagers would badly fail a hypothetical short-answer or essay test of their own faith tradition. Learning, understanding, and embracing the correct belief system for their faith does not seem to be a high priority for most adolescents or their parents (137).

One can gauge people's interest in different matters by tracking their use of language, words, or phrases? This method was used in the research project. The researchers examined the interview transcripts and systematically counted the number of teenagers who made reference to specific subjects or phrases related to salvation or understanding what a personal relationship with God should look like. Relatively few teenagers made reference to a variety of historically central religious and theological ideas. The following list shows the number of teenagers who explicitly mentioned these concepts in their interviews (167).

47 – personally sinning or being a sinner

12 – religious repentance or repenting from wrongdoing

8 – righteousness, divine or human

7 – resurrection or rising again of Jesus

6 – salvation

4 – God as Trinity

3 – the grace of God

3 – honoring God in life

2 – God as holy or reflecting holiness

0 – justification or being justified

Notice that *salvation* was only mentioned six times. *Justification* was not mentioned at all. When teenagers talked about *grace* in the interview, they were usually talking about the television show "Will and Grace," not about God's grace. *Honor* was nearly always used to refer to taking honors courses or making the honor roll at school. Very rarely was "*honor* used in reference to "honoring God."

The teenagers were quick to mention general, somewhat hazy ideas about the personal benefits of being religious (168):

112 – personally feeling, being, getting, or being made happy

99 – feeling good about oneself or life

92 – feeling better about oneself or life

26 – being or feeling personally satisfied or enjoying some satisfaction in life

21 – being or feeling personally fulfilled

Remember these numbers represent the number of teenagers who used the words, not the number of times the words were used.

Note the conclusion reached by the researchers: "Again, nobody expects adolescents to be sophisticated theologians. But very few of the descriptions of personal beliefs offered by the teenagers we interviewed—especially the Christian teenagers—come close to representing marginally coherent accounts of the basic, important religious beliefs of their own faith traditions" (137).

Misunderstanding of Grace

The NSYR found that many teenagers who claim loyalty to certain religious traditions actually hold views that strongly contradict the historic standards of those traditions. One of the basics of the Christian faith that many of the teenagers in the research project failed to clearly articulate was the doctrine of salvation by grace. Historically, salvation by God's grace alone through faith and apart from any human good works has been a central Protestant conviction. However, the professions made by many teens in the survey, including conservative Protestant teens, effectively discard the essential Protestant doctrine (136).

Consider these important facts:

- Only one out of every three teenagers accepts the biblical teaching that people who do not consciously accept Jesus Christ as their Savior will be condemned to hell. This indicates that millions of youth have bought into a works-based theology or into the belief that everyone will get into heaven (universalism).
- Three out of every five teenagers included in the project believe that if a person is generally good, or does enough good things for others during his or her life, he or she will earn a place in heaven.
- Amazingly, even though they have personally prayed to accept Jesus Christ as their Savior, half of all born-again teenagers believe that a person can earn his or her way into heaven. The evangelistic fervor of the body of believers is tempered by the fact that one-third (32 percent) of these youth reject the inevitability of condemnation for those who do not accept Jesus as their Savior.[3]

The Mandate to Spiritually Impact Children and Teenagers

In the Judeo-Christian tradition, the command to teach one's children about God reaches far back into the history of God's people. When Moses spoke to his people about entering the promised land, he told them they were to keep alive the story of how God had led them out of Egyptian slavery. They were to tell of how God promised to bless His people. Moses' instructions were clear: They were to teach these commands and promises to their children at home.

How were they to accomplish this? Through conversation, symbol, and ritual.[4]

The Hebrew Pattern

The religious education of youth was vitally important to the Israelites. As commanded by God, Hebrew teaching included the powerful memories of the redemption of Israel from bondage in Egypt and the nation's entrance into Canaan.

The biblical evidence for religious education is staggering. Throughout biblical history, it is evident that the instruction of children began very early. Josephus also stated that in his time it was an established tradition that children begin their education at an extremely early age.[5] The Hebrews expected a child to grow and become strong, full of wisdom, and blessed by God's favor. It was the task of the parents to teach children diligently in the ways of the Lord and the traditions of God's people through which these ways were made known.[6]

The general aim of Hebrew education was: (1) the transmission of the historical heritage of the Hebrew nation, and (2) instruction in the ethical conduct of life.

Hear, O Israel: The LORD our God, the LORD is one. Love the LORD your God with all your heart and with all your soul and with all your strength. These commandments that I give you today are to be upon your hearts. Impress them on your children. Talk about them when you sit at home and when you walk along the road, when you lie down and when you get up. Tie them as symbols on your hands and bind them on your foreheads. Write them on the doorframes of your houses and on your gates (Deut. 6:4-9, NIV).

This statement of law indicates that the faith of Israel was essentially a personal one. It was a faith to be taught to the children and was to be taught and talked about in the home. Many teachings found in the Book of Proverbs affirm the instruction of youth, especially by those in authority. (For examples of such instruction, see Prov. 1:8; 2:1-5; and 3:1-4, among other passages.)

Hebrew sages insisted on the moral training of children by their parents. This training was to begin early while the child's mind was most impressionable.

The Example of Jesus

Jesus' concern for youth is reflected in Matthew 18:5-6:

> *"And whoever welcomes a little child like this in my name welcomes me. But if anyone causes one of these little ones who believe in me to sin, it would be better for him to have a large millstone hung around his neck and to be drowned in the depths of the sea"* (NIV).

Jesus saw the little ones as persons and objects of God's love. He reminded us that the child has all to learn and needs everything to be supplied. In Jesus' statement to the disciples, He told them not to neglect the spiritual welfare and needs of the young.

In the Great Commission, Jesus commanded His followers to be faithful in "teaching them to obey" the commands of Christ. Therefore, teaching is an important ministry of the church in partnership with the home. It is instruction for life. The reference in Matthew 28:20 does not reflect the simple teaching of facts; it also is a reference to teaching learners how to obey Christ.[7]

The Early Church

Acts 5:42 records that the early Christians continued daily in teaching and evangelizing. Acts 15:35 states that Paul and Barnabas, with many others, were teaching and preaching the word of the Lord in Antioch. In other words, the early church took the words of our Lord seriously and began a strong teaching ministry.

In Ephesians 6:1-4 parents again are given the primary responsibility for the education of their children. The goal for the child is one of nourishment or nurture, leading to maturity and fulfillment. It has been suggested that these verses indicate how parents should give their offspring a living example. By their own personal patterns, parents can teach their children to devote themselves to studying and obeying the Scriptures from the earliest ages.

Second Timothy 2:2 is a prime illustration of the need for a strong youth ministry and for the communication of biblical truth from one life to another. The relationship of the Apostle Paul to Timothy is a good example of how effective the mentoring process can be within Christian education. Younger believers need older friends who are willing to share their experience and deepest insights. This role can be filled by a parent, a youth minister, or some other significant adult in the life of an individual teenager.

In 2 Timothy 3:14-17, Paul reminded Timothy of the faith he had been taught from his childhood. If early training in the Christian faith resulted in the spiritual strength of Timothy, surely early training can prove beneficial to today's teenagers.

The Central Role of Parents

Thus, according to Scripture, parents are to be the primary religious educators of their children. Martin Luther in his sermon "The Estate of Marriage" reflected his convictions about the role of father and mother in these words:

> Most certainly father and mother are apostles, bishops, and priests to their children, for it is they who make them acquainted with the gospel. In short there is no greater or nobler authority on earth than that of parents over their children, for this authority is both spiritual and temporal.[8]

Included in that responsibility is the necessity of teaching how one becomes a Christian. Children who are not correctly grounded in Scripture will tend to make up their own beliefs about how to obtain peace with God. Parents must not depend on others to take their role in the religious education process.

Unfortunately, statistics indicate that an increasing number of parents—mothers and fathers alike—have renounced their responsibilities to be spiritual leaders in the home. This lack of responsibility obviously comes at a high cost to the children who are being neglected. This abdication also causes problems for society as a whole.[9]

This glaring, spiritual problem places pressure on youth ministers to develop a well-balanced program that includes evangelism, discipleship, and ministry, along with fellowship and worship. Youth ministers may want to consider creating a parent ministry or a parent mentor program that will instruct parents in how to carry out their spiritual leadership roles in the home. Youth ministers also cannot afford to assume that teenagers are hearing the gospel at home. Therefore, youth ministry must be prepared to assume a back-up role. While helping parents encourage spiritual transformation at home, youth leaders also can provide a solid source of biblical truth outside the home.

Consider the following:
- Parents who do not teach what Scripture says about salvation almost guarantee that their teenagers will simply make up their own ideas.
- Teenagers who make up and trust their own ideas about salvation likely never will be saved.
- Teenagers who possibly come from Christian homes who never are saved will spend eternity in hell.

The stakes could not be higher!

What Teenagers Must Do to Be Saved

Parents primarily and church leaders secondarily must communicate the following to lost teenagers.

You are important to God. Before God created the world, He worked out a plan to set you in right relation with Him. Why did He do this? Because He loves you and wants you to enjoy the best life possible. How can you enjoy God's good life for you? One way to find out is to follow what is called the Roman Road. The Roman Road is a group of verses found in the Book of Romans. By following the Roman Road, you can learn about God's plan of salvation. You can also use the Roman Road to show someone you know how to accept Jesus as Lord and Savior.

The Roman Road

1. WE ARE ALL SINNERS.

Romans 3:10-12, 23

¹⁰ *As it is written:*
    "There is no one righteous, not even one;
¹¹ *there is no one who understands,*
    no one who seeks God.
¹² *All have turned away,*
    together they have become useless;
    there is no one who does good,
    there is not even one."
²³ *for all have sinned and fall short of the glory of God.*

2. THE PENALTY FOR SIN.

Romans 6:23

²³ *For the wages of sin is death, but the gift of God is eternal life in Christ Jesus our Lord.*

3. THE PAYMENT GOD MADE FOR OUR SIN.

Romans 5:8-9—

⁸ *But God proves his own love for us in that while we were still sinners Christ died for us.*
⁹ *Much more then, since we have now been declared righteous by His blood, we will be saved through Him from wrath.*

4. CONFESS JESUS AS LORD. ASK GOD TO SAVE YOU.

Romans 10:9-10,13—

⁹ *If you confess with your mouth, "Jesus is Lord," and believe in your heart that God raised Him from the dead, you will be saved.* ¹⁰ *With the heart one believes, resulting in righteousness, and with the mouth one confesses, resulting in salvation.*
¹³ *For everyone who calls on the name of the Lord will be saved.*

5. Read the following prayer:

How to ask God to save you—
Dear God: I know You love me. I realize I am a sinner. I have not lived as You
have wanted me to live. I believe Your Son, Jesus, died for me on the cross and
was raised from death to provide forgiveness and eternal life. Please save me
as I turn from my sins, place my faith in Jesus, and receive Him as Lord and
Savior. I will no longer live according to my selfish desires and plans, but will
follow Your desires and plans for my life. Thank You for saving me and giving
me eternal life. I pray this prayer in Jesus' name. Amen.[10]

Parenting Children by Grace

The style parents choose to raise children also can help move those children toward a personal relationship with Jesus Christ. It is much easier to grasp the grace of God when children live with parents who relate to them in grace. Conversely, it is very difficult for teenagers to imagine how Almighty God can be grace-filled when they seldom have seen that quality of grace expressed at home. As writer Tim Kimmel has pointed out, "Grace is not so much what we do as parents, but how we do what we do. Grace is the best advertisement for a personal relationship with the living God."[11]

Pray

Praying for the salvation of children is the highest privilege and gravest responsibility of parents and church leaders. Teaching children the basics of the faith is vital. Parenting in a grace-filled way is vital. Inviting children to salvation is vital. But arching over all these duties is the duty to pray without ceasing.

The enemy knows the name of every child. The roaring lion intends to devour each one while on earth, and he intends to do his worst to each one for eternity. Christian parents and leaders absolutely must lift up their voices before daybreak, calling out to the Savior to rescue their children. Nothing else matters as much.

Results of Matt's Evaluation

As Matt reviewed the numerical success of the youth ministry he directs, he became aware of the need to encourage, equip, and empower the parents of the church's teenagers to minister to their own children. This should begin with showing parents how to lead their children to a personal relationship with Christ, followed by instruction on nurturing those teenagers toward continued spiritual growth. As Matt resolved to enlarge the church's ministry to include parents as his allies, he felt that the youth group would develop a spiritual dimension that would lead to greater ministry fulfillment.

53

ENDNOTES

1. Tokunboh Adeyemo quoted in Robert E. Webber, *Ancient-Future Evangelism: Making Your Church a Faith-Forming Community* (Baker Books, Grand Rapids, 2003), 13.

2. Christian Smith, *Soul Searching, The Religious and Spiritual Lives of American Teenagers* (Oxford University Press, New York, 2005), 120. Throughout this and other chapters, numbers in parentheses also represent page numbers from *Soul Searching*.

3. George Barna, *Real Teens: A Contemporary Snapshot of Youth Culture* (Regal, Ventura, 2001), 126.

4. Merton P. Strommen and A. Irene Strommen, *Five Cries of Parents* (Harper & Row, San Francisco, 1985), 130.

5. J. Kaster, "Education, OT," *The Interpreter's Dictionary of the Bible*, E-J (Abington Press, Nashville, 1962), 33.

6. O. J. Baab, "Child," *The Interpreter's Dictionary of the Bible*, A-D (Abington Press, Nashville, 1962), 558. Examples include Deuteronomy 4:9-10; 6:7, 21; 11:19; 31:12-13; Joshua 4:6-7; Psalm 78:4.

7. Frank Stagg, *New Testament Theology* (Broadman Press, Nashville, 1962), 273.

8. Martin Luther, "The Estate of Marriage," *Luther's Works* 45, 1958, 45 quoted in Merton P. Strommen and Richard A. Hardel, *Passing on the Faith: A Radical New Model for Youth and Family Ministry* (Saint Mary's Press, Christian Brothers Publications, Winona, MN, 2000), 28.

9. Strommen and Hardel, 29.

10. *DiscipleYouth Bible* (Holman Bible Publishers, Nashville, 1985), 5a.

11. Tim Kimmel, *Grace Based Parenting* (Word Publishing, Nashville, 2004), 35.

CHAPTER FIVE

The Adults Teenagers Need

THE RESEARCH

Roger Glidewell

54

IWAS IN THE MIDDLE OF A CLASS LECTURE that morning at the university where I teach. The class was studying God's eternal purpose for humanity. As we studied God's promise to "bless all peoples" through Abram in Genesis 12, we were reminded that God's eternal purpose is the only certainty in life. As humans, we must choose whether we are going to trust in His purpose or rebel against it.

It was at that moment that a fellow instructor knocked on my door to tell me the horrifying news: the towers of the World Trade Center in New York had been hit by commercial airplanes.

The date was September 11, 2001.

We sat in sickened silence. At that moment, we clung to the hope that God was—despite the choices of humans bent on evil—in control.

The cloud of dust that rose over New York that sad day is somehow symbolic of the cloud of doubt and uncertainty that has destroyed many presuppositions about our world. How will we raise up a generation of faithful teenagers to meet the unique challenges that face them today? Every generation has its hurdles, but none before our own has had to deal with so many that seem so high!

This Generation

Every previous generation of young believers:

- *has encountered the horrors of war.* But this generation of teenagers has grown up in a world in which a murky new kind of war—terrorism—is being waged on a global scale with no end in sight;
- *has struggled with sexual temptation.* But this generation has visual images of graphic sex coming at them from every angle including through the internet and other media;

- *has suffered persecution for the faith.* But this generation faces a monumental wave of secularization and anti-Christian sentiment.

The problems of past generations have been numerous and intense, but this generation must learn to deal with challenges that are global rather than local, continuous rather than intermittent, invasive rather than isolated. Our world has now truly become a global community, with both new possibilities and pressures unlike any other confronting the rising generation of teenagers.

In this complicated environment, many parents doubt whether they have much influence on their adolescent children. Their doubts are enhanced by the increasing speed of life. Globe-sized events seem to overwhelm us, and technology has eclipsed parents as the repository of knowledge for many teens.

Peer Pressure versus Parent Influence

On the surface, the "youth subculture" seems to have more influence than adults with teenagers. In previous generations, adult authority figures—especially parents—were clearly the primary influencers of young people. Moms spent time with their daughters in the kitchen. Dads worked side-by-side with their sons in the field all day, every day.

But the pressures created by our consumer society have separated first dads and then moms from that level of interaction with their children. Now, other teenagers and the teen subculture seem to have usurped parents' privileged position as dominant source of influence and impact for teenagers.

Any shopping trip with a teenager demonstrates that trend. Teens seem to have a homing device that picks up on what's "in" and what's "not" among their peers. Even though they claim to be independent of external influences, teens often express their individuality by dressing the same, getting piercings that are the same, and being tattooed to look the same as other teens with whom they associate!

In other words, even their independent thinking is dependent upon the influence of their peers. This leaves us to wonder if peers or parents really have the inside track when it comes to shaping the way teenagers live and the choices they make. We know that teenagers are greatly influenced by peer pressure, and we wonder as adults whether we can compete in the marketplace of teenage values, which seem far more "flexible" than those of their elders.

Not long ago I spoke at a youth conference on the dangers of "tolerance." I reminded listeners that the church is harmed when believers passively tolerate certain sinful behaviors in society at large. Worse still, unbelievers may assume that their actions will not result in negative consequences—including eternal separation from God.

At the conclusion of the meeting, a small group of teenagers—all dressed in black—sought me out to talk further. It was pretty obvious that they had a different view of life. One girl said, "My best friend is a lesbian, and she acts better than most Christians I know." I asked the girl if she was a believer, and she looked pained that I would even ask. "Of course," she said.

I then asked if she had told her lesbian friend about Jesus, and she emphatically told me that she didn't push her religion on her friends.

"I wouldn't want you to be my friend," I told her. Amazed, she asked why.

"Because you would allow me to go to hell in the name of tolerance," I said. "Best friends rescue best friends from danger, but you tolerate potential harm for your friends without even pointing them to the hope or help offered through Christ. I wouldn't feel safe with you as my friend because you are more interested in having friends than in being one."

These teenagers had clearly opted for the secular message of inclusion with few—if any—boundaries on what was acceptable or unacceptable behavior. They had accepted the mantra "to each his own" without giving it a second thought. The interesting thing about these teens' "tolerance" was that they professed tolerance for other people's opinions, but they themselves obviously had an unwritten dress code and were very intolerant of anyone who did not agree with them. Each of them had sacrificed their independence to gain acceptance by the group.

Tolerant? No. Independent thinkers? I don't think so.

Obviously, teenagers seek the approval of other teens, and they are greatly influenced by their peers. But is that the end of the story? Should parents and other adults simply abdicate influence to the subculture and the powerful media engine that seems to drive teens ever further away from parental influence? The answer to that question just might surprise you.

For Better or for Worse...Teens Prefer Adult Guidance

There is hope for parents and adults in the church who feel overwhelmed by the powerful forces that seem determined to separate their teenagers from their influence. The aura of teenagers' independence from any influences outside their own youth subculture may not be as strong or as permanent as it seems. Recent research has indicated that, for better or worse, teenagers still look to significant adults when they need a role model. In fact, in the National Study of Youth and Religion survey, more than two-thirds of Southern Baptist teenagers indicated that the two most important factors in their decision-making processes are advice from an adult and Scripture.

Teens turn elsewhere for help only when a vacuum is created by the absence of meaningful relationships with adults. In *New Directions for Youth Ministry*, Wayne Rice wrote: "The peer group exerts a powerful influence on millions of kids today, but it's only influence by default. It's influence given to it by a culture that has abandoned its young. But when parents are there for their kids—and when teenagers are surrounded by adults who truly care about them—the peer group is virtually de-fanged. It and the media are stripped of their power over kids."[1]

Adult absenteeism in the lives of teenagers has created a vacancy in the position of "authoritative and reliable source of truth" among teenagers. Rather than the teenagers rejecting adults, it is the adults in our culture who have abandoned teenagers.

Adults Greatly Influence Teens...Today!

Teens' preference for adults to help them steer a course for life is not so difficult to understand. They are looking for guidance and assurance for the future. They are asking, *Who am I? Where do I belong? How can I make a meaningful contribution to life?* For answers to these questions they turn to those whom they believe should have answers—their elders. They view adults—not peers—as the most informed answer-givers, and adults with whom they are closest are their most trustworthy answer-givers.

Teens are especially eager to hear positive insights about their worth and potential from significant adults in their lives. As a veteran youth leader, I have found that even teens who are otherwise distracted suddenly become extremely focused when I have spoken words of personal encouragement to them. In fact, sometimes their whole countenance has changed, and their eyes have come into sharp focus when the subject turns to their potential and worth as individuals. The only word to describe it is "hunger."

Teenagers not only hunger for adult insight and direction regarding the future, they also look to adults to serve as appropriate role models for the present. Teenagers imitate the behaviors of adults when they deem those adults worthy of emulation. A teenager's opinion of himself often mirrors the opinions of others, especially that of adults he views as significant. Teenagers' behavior almost shouts to important adults in their world, "I am who you think I am."

If they don't get words of encouragement from adults who are close to them, they will seek hope elsewhere: movie actors, music stars, athletes, and others whom the culture has granted a platform whether they deserve one or not.

Quantity Time Counts, Too!

But in the battle for influence with teens, it is parents, teachers, coaches, and youth leaders who have the advantage over star power, affluence, or prestige. The closer the emotional ties between teenagers and their adult role models, the more likely it is that the teenagers will imitate those adults. And spending personal time is adults' "special ingredient" to gain their teens' respect and trust. When it comes to spending time with teens, more is better!

Many studies have documented the link between parental supervision and the behavior of teenagers. Josh McDowell has conducted research on the connection between at-risk behaviors and the relationships children have with their parents. He stated that, "Two major studies of churched teenagers commissioned first in 1987 and again in 1994 (found that) the closer teenagers are to their parents relationally, the less at risk they are to unacceptable behavior." McDowell went on to add that "every major sociological study of the last 15 years which cross-tabulates human relationships or lack of them with human behavior reveals that the more disconnected a person is relationally, the more prone he or she is to engage in anti-social behavior."[2]

The White House Conference on Teenagers concluded that "Parental involvement is a major influence in helping teens avoid risks such as smoking, drinking, drug use, sexual activity, violence, and suicide attempts, while increasing educational achievement and expected attainment."[3]

A YMCA survey concluded that 94 percent of parents believe children learn values at home. Not surprisingly, 80 percent of the children agreed.[4] Southern Baptist teenagers in the NSYR revealed that the more time a parent or other significant adult spends with a teen, the more likely that teen will follow that adult's advice. SBC teens who say they are "very close" to their mother are also the teens who have spent time engaged in activities with Mom. For example, approximately 71 percent of these teens say they attend concerts or plays together; 86 percent say they have fixed something together; and a whopping 91 percent say they have exercised or played games or sports together. Southern Baptist teens who say they have "hung out" with their dads fairly often have also engaged in extracurricular activities together, such as fixing something with their dad (85 percent) or playing a game or sport with their dad (86 percent).

Even the number of meals shared with adults is an indicator of the powerful influence of spending time with teenagers. In homes where families share meals together, teenagers listen and follow the advice of parents more closely! According to the White House Report on Teenagers, "Having a close relationship with one's children and spending time with them, for example having dinner together on a regular basis, is strongly related to whether teens engage in risky behavior such as drinking, fighting, or having sex at early ages."[5]

Spending time with adults in church also makes a difference to teens. When other adults in the church assist parents by spending time with teenagers, the results are encouraging: 58 percent of SBC teens are "very comfortable" talking with adult youth leaders in their church about their concerns. Nearly 70 percent of Southern Baptist teenagers in the NSYR said that there were adults at church with whom they enjoyed talking about their concerns.

In fact, teenagers themselves say that church is a good place to talk about serious issues, and they feel safe there to discuss the challenges they face.

But Does Quantity Equal Quality?

So for parents who have spent time with their children and have involved them in church activities, the chances of raising their teens to be spiritually mature adults appear encouraging, right? Sort of. But we shouldn't break out the salsa and chips or start the celebration just yet.

To say that the kids of religious parents usually adopt their parents' faith tells only half the story. For a clearer understanding of what this means we must first ask, "What kind of religious values are the parents modeling?" The quality of significant adults' faith does make a difference in the lives of their teens.

When I was a teenager, a youth leader asked me, "If you were growing up in a Muslim household, would you have become a Christian?" I indignantly responded, "Yes, I would have become a Christian!" But truthfully, his challenge to my comfortable assumption struck home. I had embraced Christianity while in elementary school, making a "personal decision" that I assumed was independent of others' influence. But was it?

To be completely truthful, I had been influenced by the faith of the adults in my world. I had become a Christian because the only two options that seemed available to me as a child were Christianity or atheism. Hey, even as a little kid I knew that *the fool says in his heart, God does not exist*" (Ps. 14:1).

Bottom line: I chose the path with which I was most comfortable, and I had adopted the faith of the adult world in which I grew up. I was a product of my environment. It would be years before I would be confronted with options other than Christianity. Many teenagers follow this same path. Just like me, they are far more influenced by their environment than they realize; and they usually adopt the values of their elders.

This can be either good news or bad news. When parents have a relationship with God that is real and genuine, this loving relationship with their Heavenly Father often parallels the manner in which they relate as father (and mother) to their own children. In the NSYR survey, the link between parents' devotion to God and devotion to their children was obvious: When parents attend church services more than once a week and also "hang out" with their teens by participating in sports, playing games, or fixing things together, their teens are far more likely to adopt positive views on strong religious values.

However, when parents and significant adults fail to combine a devotion to their children with a true devotion to God, children may adopt a casual—or even negative—attitude toward religious faith. The NSYR reveals that when faith is extremely important to a parent, it also will be important to their children.

Some church-going parents assume God exists but is basically uninvolved in their personal lives. In turn, they convey this perception of God to their teens, apart from the scrutiny of the congregation. As a result, this distance from God may be echoed in their own relationship with their teens.

Other church-going parents and adults convey the idea that God is there for individuals rather than individuals being there for Him. They only appeal to God when they think a situation is beyond their control. For example, parents will pray—when their child comes up to bat! They will bring their kids to church—but only to aid them with discipline at home. Their objective seems to be to get God to do something to benefit their kingdom rather than motivating themselves to do something for His kingdom. Their personal relationship with God is distant and mechanical at best.

When adult behaviors fail to reflect their stated belief system, teenagers become discouraged. Parents' devotion toward their kids must be combined with a devotion toward God if they are to be as effective as possible in raising teenagers who develop a mature faith.

Recently I was talking with a young person at a camp. We were having a casual conversation while walking to the dining hall. I asked him how he was doing. "All right, for now" was all he said.

Curious, I asked what he meant by that. That was when he dropped the bombshell: "My parents are sleeping in separate beds." I was caught completely by surprise (and I thought I was past being surprised at teenagers' comments!).

"Everyone thinks my family is so great," he went on. "But my mom caught my dad with another woman, and now she knows why they haven't had sex in years."

I didn't speak. How does one respond to that? I just nodded my head.

"My parents work with the youth group at church," he said. "The kids don't know anything is going on. When the youth group comes over to the house, my parents act like everything is OK. No one knows. But I and my brother and sisters know. Nothing is the same anymore. We used to be a family, but not now. I'm thinking about leaving home

61

when this camp is over."

And what about his relationship with God? He wouldn't say.

We don't really fool our own children. They see their parents in all types of situations, and they can tell whether their parents are being consistent or inconsistent, real or fake. They also know if their parents' relationship with God is authentic and worth emulating or not. If it's not, their willingness to embrace their parents' faith is compromised.

When I was asked as a teen whether I would have become a Christian had I been raised in a Muslim home, a more honest answer most likely would have been *no*. In all likelihood I would have become a Muslim just like my parents. But the real "kicker" in this equation is, *What kind of Muslim would I have become as an adult? A Muslim in name only? A devoted adherent? Or maybe an angry, passionate terrorist?* The quality of my relationship with meaningful adults would have contributed greatly to the degree of my religious values.

When Christian parents and other adult role models fail to pass on meaningful faith to their children in an environment of close relationships, the fallout is stark. Their children fail to see the significance of religion as practiced by their parents. They may drop out—physically or at least emotionally—from church participation even while they are still young.

Adults Impact Teens—Tomorrow As Well As Today

What's even more important, adult influence on teenagers will carry over into those teenagers' religious values later as adults. If teens who have dropped out of church return as adults, it may be for instrumentalist reasons like that of their elders. The relational bond parents create with their children affects teenagers' current beliefs and behaviors, but they also help shape their future belief systems! The future faith of teens is carried on the wings of current relationships with significant adults.

This axiom is evident in our own experience as parents and youth leaders. Many of us, who as teenagers vehemently insisted, "I'll never become like my parents," ended up doing just that! We became far more like our parents than we ever intended. Think of the times we have heard someone exclaim, "You look (or act) just like your dad (or mom)," while pointing out some mannerism we have picked up from a parent—probably the mannerism we most dislike!

We almost unconsciously pick up our parents' voice inflections, their facial or verbal expressions, their attitudes, their posture, even their gait. These characteristics may not surface for years, but eventually we catch ourselves doing and saying things that look and sound like our parents! Truly, we become like those who were closest to us in our childhood.

In the end, it is the parents and significant adults in the lives of teenagers whose influence prevails, especially later in life. Peers' influence on the religious and moral development of youth may be far more temporary than we think. Instead, as teens move beyond their high school years, they revert more and more to the fundamental values they learned from their parents and valued adults.

But What About the Youth Ministry?

As noted, teenagers' adult faith systems are more likely to reflect what was demonstrated by significant adults in their lives, especially the ones at home, rather than what they saw in their teenage peers. Their primal convictions re-emerge only after they have left the social environment provided by the church youth group. Sadly, many teenagers use the youth group more as a source of social gatherings rather than spiritual growth. Consequently, it is only after graduation that their true faith becomes apparent. After graduating, teenagers who were formerly very active in the youth group often revert to their elders' patterns.

Even adult youth leaders in the church may mistakenly equate a teen-ager's participation in church activities with spiritual conviction when, in fact, it may be more about social convenience. We cannot judge the spiritual values of teenagers only by their current level of youth group participation—even when that student's participation seems to exceed the spiritual maturity of his or her parents.

Once the teenager graduates and moves beyond the social "bubble" of the youth group, his or her attitude about religion likely will swing back toward the basic values of his elders. While the youth group may have provided a wonderful social environment with other students, it may not have provided the kind of true spiritual nurture that sustains a student outside the immediate context of the youth group.

To demonstrate this, all we have to do is look at the data regarding where students are only one year after graduation from high school. In his research, Josh McDowell found that 88 percent of teenagers in churches graduate and never return to the church.[6] In a survey of religious teenagers, McDowell asked this question: *What part will God and church play in your life after you leave high school?* Over several decades of surveys, between 44 and 66 percent of teenagers have responded that religion will play a very strong role in their lives. But in this more recent survey, the percentage has dropped to 33 percent.[7]

Churches today cannot expect to see teenagers automatically return to the church after they are married and start having children. While their elders in the buster generation followed this trend, only 16 percent of teenagers who are nonattending SBC students said they would attend religious services when they are age 25. In contrast, sociologist Wesley Perkins' study of college students found that 69 percent of students with two highly religious parents reported a strong personal faith and remained spiritually active apart from their parents.[8] This indicates that parental and adult influence—rather than the level of church activity—serves as a strong determining factor in a student's decision to remain active in church after leaving the youth group.

Over my years of youth ministry, I have come to realize that one youth leader—no matter how effective he or she may be—cannot effectively relate to an infinite number of teenagers. An effective youth ministry, then, cannot overlook the most important asset available in shaping young people's lives—their parents and other significant adults in the church whose lives become a testimony to the love of God.

Josh McDowell has done some research on young Christians in America. His recent research has led him to conclude that, "In essence what you believe by the time you are 13 is what you will die believing."[9] If that is true, it reinforces the truth that most teenagers are largely influenced more by adults—especially parents—than by their peers, even the peers in the church youth group.

Speaking to a group of youth leaders, McDowell said, "It comes down to relationships, starting with parents. The number one job description of a youth minister should not be to teach truth or lead worship or discipleship, but to help parents relate to their kids."[10]

As youth leaders, we must recognize that enlisting the participation of adults in youth ministry may be the most valuable contribution we can make to our teenagers. All adults in the church should be reminded that we are held accountable in heaven for our influence with teenagers. To use that influence for kingdom work among teenagers is to be regarded as a supreme privilege!

While we are ministering to teenagers, we should keep in mind that they are becoming people of influence themselves. I always wonder, *Which one of the students in this group of teenagers is going to be the next Billy Graham?* When they are teenagers, it can be difficult to imagine how any of them will have a positive impact for the kingdom of God, but the one you least expect might just emerge as a powerful leader if shown the right role models for his or her life.

Over the years the students in my charge have grown up to become contemporary music artists, preachers, youth ministers, missionaries, actors, athletes, politicians, artists, and even a Miss America. Simply by being their youth leader, I became partly accountable for their spiritual nurture. Of course, I have had very little to do with the future success of any of the remarkable teenagers who have passed through youth groups I have served; but I must always assume that I and the other significant adults in their lives have played a powerful role in shaping whether they experience a lifetime walk with Jesus Christ.

The truth is, even though an adult may be graying, overweight, and clueless about the Internet, he or she can be significant in molding the lives of teenagers. What a tragedy it would be to miss that!

THE IMPLICATIONS

Mike Landrum

The first half of this chapter has established that adults are important to teenagers. To prosper as Christians, teens need to be connected with godly adults inside and outside the home. Parents and church leaders need to lock arms in the enterprise to "present everyone perfect in Christ" (Col. 1:28, NIV). We need to give careful attention to the ways adult leaders and parents can maximize their effectiveness.

Adult Leadership
Generally speaking, teenagers need all kinds of adults in their lives. A wise leader does not surround himself with a team of people who are

clones. Instead, a wise leader surrounds himself with a team of people rich in variety.

A Variety of Leaders

At one point in my ministry, I served on a church staff with five ministers. Each minister had a different task. Problems emerged when we came together in one room at the same time because the pastor had surrounded himself with four other people just like himself. The environment created by a team of domineering, type "A" personalities who always thought they were right usually led to war more times than to peace. Almost without exception, one of us would leave a staff meeting "bleeding" emotionally from the conflict. A better team would have been balanced in temperament, personality, giftedness, and leadership styles. It is a good thing for teenagers to have that kind of variety when it comes to the adults in their lives.

Examining the teenage phenomenon of "dating" may lend some credence to the wisdom of variety. The dating process gives young people the opportunity to discern whom they *don't* want to marry as much as whom they *do* want to marry. Discovering areas of incompatibility early on can help them enjoy a more blissful marriage later.

Identifying significant adults for student ministry is a vital practice. Youth leaders should celebrate the variety of people, personalities, and giftedness in the kingdom of God and should find ways to integrate those differences into appropriate ministry opportunities. Youth can benefit tremendously from the experiences and advice available from a wide variety of individuals.

Even more important than the things that set leaders apart is what should unify them—a call from God to work with youth. When identifying leaders, one cannot overlook or presume upon the call. Likewise, potential leaders should be encouraged to examine their own call carefully to avoid being placed in a ministry outside their calling.

No youth minister should ever believe, *I'm all these kids need*. From the first day he arrives at a church, the youth minister should work at building an increasingly large and spiritually-transformed group of leaders. That group of leaders should strive to become a rich spiritual resource for the teenagers with whom they work by nurturing their own spiritual health and growth.

COMFORT LEVELS

A primary quality needed to minister to teenagers effectively is a high degree of comfort. Teenagers were asked if "adults at church were very or somewhat easy to talk to or know." The Southern Baptist response was an astounding 86 percent. The response from all youth in the survey was equally telling at 80 percent. Teenagers need adults who make them feel comfortable because a high comfort level can facilitate life change. How can an adult leader do this? Let's explore three possibilities.

1. *Relational Ministry.* We can help students feel comfortable around us by being vulnerable in our relationships. What we are really talking about here is relational ministry. There are three levels of relational ministry: impress, influence, and impact. If you want to *impress* me, send a famous expert (like Toby Mac in music or Barry Bonds for baseball) into the room. This requires no relationship, just visible presence. Impression is usually momentary and emotional.

   Influence requires some relationship. I can be influenced to eat Mexican food or I can be influenced to eat Italian food. I can influence you about the person for whom you should vote in an election. I can use my influence in many ways, but a certain amount of relationship is required for influence to occur.

   Depth is not a characteristic of this level of relationship. While influence lasts longer than impression, it can be built on very shallow interaction. What tends to keep the influence alive is not the depth of the relationship, but the exposure to the relationship. Using track terminology, influence does not need a marathon. Short, 50-yard sprints will do if they are consistent.

   In contrast, making an *impact* on the life of someone else requires an ongoing, intimate relationship. Impact is all about investment because it is about changing lives. It is the marathon—a commitment made for the long haul.

   The lasting effect of impact can be seen and felt for many years. Paul told Timothy that *"the things you have heard me say in the presence of many witnesses entrust to reliable men who will also be qualified to teach others"* (2 Tim. 2:2, NIV).

   If you throw a rock into a pond, the reverberations can be seen from a distance and felt across the water. The sizes of the rock and the body of water affect the depth of impact. Vulnerable and in-depth relationships are more likely to produce life change (impact) that will be felt in a student's life now, and potentially, forever. This is the ministry level we should strive to move toward with our teenagers and leaders.

Many people have shaped my life over the years. One significant adult during my adolescence was Shorty. His real name was Buford, but everyone called him Shorty because he was only about five feet tall. He may have been short in physical stature, but he was mighty when it came to loving Jesus and loving me. He invested himself in me during some difficult and joyous times of my teenage years.

When I needed a ride to church, Shorty was there. When I needed someone to talk with, Shorty was there. When I needed to cry or express frustration and anger, Shorty was there. When I had victories to share, Shorty was there. He loved me as I was. He also allowed me to see his pain, joy, and struggles because his life was an open book. As I read that "book" over the years, I saw Jesus over and over again. Shorty made me feel comfortable by sharing his life with me. He was vulnerable.

As we relate to teenagers, we need to help them feel comfortable around us. The responsibility to model this example for adult leadership falls to the youth minister. If the student minister fails in this, the proper level of comfort—also known as a ministry of presence—will not exist. The research and my experience confirm this truth.

According to the NSYR statistics, 78 percent of the SBC teenagers surveyed and 79 percent of all teenagers surveyed said they have adults in their congregation other than family members with whom they enjoy talking and who give encouragement. Additionally, 75 percent of SBC teenagers who do not have that kind of relationship with a significant adult would like to have one. Adults who will listen to and talk with teenagers are wanted and needed. How do we minister to teenagers? Develop a relationship with them and live like Jesus in front of them.

Laugh with teenagers, and let teenagers laugh at you. This kind of investment takes time. Adult leaders will have to "hang out" with teens—and not just on our turf, such as the church building or at a scheduled program. We must hang out on their turf, wherever that may be. Laughing together involves sharing time and common experiences. Sharing those experiences (and being able to laugh about them later) allows us to drop our masks and show teenagers who we really are.

Teenagers need adults who display a reasonable degree of transparency. They need adults who will be honest. Even if leaders do not share everything, they know what is appropriate and what can be most meaningful for youth. This may require a certain level of risk, but it is a risk wise adult leaders are willing to take.

2. *Love and Acceptance.* A second trait needed by adult leaders to help teenagers feel comfortable for the purpose of ministry is love and acceptance. God will not love me any more tomorrow than He loves me today. He is the only Person I know with that capacity, but teenagers need to know that kind of love. God's love reaches beyond the parameters of depravity and accepts us as we are. Often, God chooses to use significant adults to portray that love to teenagers.

God invested in us through Jesus, knowing what we could become as He changes our lives. The Holy Spirit is at work developing our sanctification. Adults who work with teenagers need to love them as the Father loves them. For some this could mean dealing with their own pride, selfishness, or prejudices. It is impossible to love others intimately until we feel and acknowledge the love of God in our lives.

Adult leaders must deal with their own self-image problems in order to minister more effectively to teenagers. It will be hard to love some students until you remember how Christ loves you unconditionally. This also means we cannot use teenagers to meet our emotional or spiritual needs. Our healthy self-identity can be a useful tool in the hands of the Holy Spirit. Healthy adult leaders enable healthy student ministry because their focus is not on their own needs, but on the power of God. It is through His power that the needs of teenagers then can be met appropriately.

Love and acceptance directed toward teenagers becomes much easier when our self image and security rests in our personal relationship with Christ. Living out a healthy relationship with Jesus provides credibility and creates an atmosphere conducive to "conversational confrontation." Loving teenagers with their frailties is easier when we know God loves us with our frailties.

3. *Life of Integrity in Christ.* Is it important to live as a positive, godly example for the teenagers we seek to reach? If there were any doubt, I think the first half of this chapter has adequately helped us answer this question. Yes! It is important!

Of the Southern Baptist teenagers surveyed, 68 percent of them have adults in their lives to turn to for support, advice, and help who are part of their religious congregation or youth group. *Hallelujah!* for that 68 percent, but what about the other 32 percent? Every student needs adults in their lives. So when we are present, how important are our lifestyles? How important is our integrity?

The adult leader must first and foremost model and present Christ, not just a church program or idea. I am not belittling programs, but they will not change a life by themselves. They are simply tools God uses to transform lives. According to Scripture, a personal relationship with Jesus is the only thing that has the power to change a heart.

I had a parent approach me the first week I was on the field at a new church as the student minister.

"I am so glad you are here," she told me. "I want you to help me get little Johnny in church. He's not in church. He doesn't like to come. I believe if we have a youth program, he will come. I know you will have some wonderful activities, programs, and trips."

I let this dear lady wax on for about five minutes, but my response made her jaw drop.

"I don't want to get your son involved in church," I told her.

"I can't believe you said that," she told me. "You are the youth pastor. You are supposed to want kids to be in church. That is what we hired you for. Maybe you should be fired before you get started."

When I felt like I had her attention, I said, "I don't want to get your son involved in church programs and activities. I want to get him involved with a relationship with Jesus. If he and Jesus begin a relationship, then the problem doesn't exist."

As adult leaders, we want to get teenagers involved in a relationship with Jesus. If we win them on our personalities, we have to keep them with our personalities. If we win them on basketball, that is what it takes to keep them. But if we introduce them to Jesus and He draws them into the kingdom, He keeps them. Needless to say, this yields much better results and is more biblical.

If we want to build relationships so we can see teenagers born into God's kingdom and grow in their relationship with Jesus, our relationship with Jesus needs to be fresh and vibrant. *"Very early in the morning, while it was still dark, Jesus got up, left the house and went off to a solitary place, where he prayed"* (Mark 1:35, NIV).

The most important thing in life is a relationship with Jesus. This is our first priority relationship. The second priority is our family. The third priority in life is our job or ministry. The same is true for parents. It is important to continually develop our walk with Christ. Romans 8:29 says, *"For those God foreknew he also predestined to be conformed to the likeness of his Son, that he might be the firstborn among many brothers"* (NIV).

Adult leaders should be striving to become more like Christ. Are we "becoming" or are we "doing?" We need to be careful not to communicate—either deliberately or accidentally—that doing stuff in church is what being a Christian is all about. Our church involvement is an outflow of our walk with Jesus. The "stuff" we do is not nearly as important as our relationship with Jesus.

Youth ministers can do their teenagers a favor by teaching adult leadership this truth. The ministry they have with teenagers is not the most important relationship. It only makes it to third place. Our integrity in life and relationships is crucial to gaining credibility. Our impact in lives will be greater when His name is not just on our lips, but His nature is also in us and visible as we live our lives.

Parents

A primary group of adults needed in the lives of teenagers is parents. It is clear in Scripture that children are the responsibility of their parents.

Ephesians 6:1-3 says:
"Children, obey your parents in the Lord, for this is right. Honor your father and mother—which is the first commandment with a promise—that it may go well with you and that you may enjoy long life on the earth" (NIV).

Paul said, *"Follow my example, as I follow the example of Christ"* (1 Cor. 11:1, NIV). While Scripture does not tell us whether or not Paul was a parent, the principle can be applied to parenting. Teenagers need a positive spiritual example, and parents should strive to follow Christ in order to be a healthy spiritual example to their teens. I want to focus on three characteristics parents need to impact the lives of their teenagers.

1. *Warmth and Love.* I heard a story many years ago that I hope is not true. A couple came to the pastor for marriage counseling. It seemed to the pastor that the woman was upset because her husband never told her he loved her. She was questioning whether he really did love her and wanted to stay in the marriage. The pastor asked the husband why he would not tell his wife he loved her. He responded, "I told her once, and that ought to be good enough!"

Once is not enough in a marriage or in a parent-child relationship. We need to tell our children we love them repeatedly.

The NSYR research found that a high percentage of parents are expressing their love and acceptance to their teenagers. Of the teenagers surveyed, 83 percent believe their parents love them and accept them for who they are. The statistic is 10 percent higher among "devoted" types. That is a lot of love expressed!

2. *Physical Touch.* I grew up in a divorced family, and I lived with my dad and step-mom. She became "Mom" when I was five years old, so she was the only mom figure I knew growing up. Mom and I would kiss and hug each other. This was a natural and frequent occurrence. But my dad and I very rarely kissed and hugged. It was an awkward thing for him. This has influenced my habits as a father. I wanted my son to grow up hugging and kissing on Dad as a natural occurrence. I needed and wanted the security from my dad that positive physical touch can provide in a parent-child relationship.

Teenagers need parents who express love to them. Parents need to say it and express it. Is it really love if not expressed? Twenty-five percent of teenagers say their mom never, rarely, or sometimes hugs them. Thirty-nine percent of teenagers say their dad never, rarely, or sometimes hugs them.

There is a lot of "bad" touch in our world. Child abuse, pornography, sexual molestation, and rape all represent this reality. As Christian people, we need to engage in appropriate, "positive" touch. Wisdom certainly should be practiced concerning this subject, but parents hold the key to making sure teenagers get what they need in this area of life.

Youth leaders can challenge parents to show healthy physical affection to children from the moment they are born. Parents also can be encouraged to hug their kids several times a day. This modeling will not only benefit their children, but it can serve as a positive example for other parents who struggle with showing love and affection.

3. *Time.* The cliché is old but true: "Love is spelled TIME." I am amazed by the research that reveals only 70 percent of teenagers felt their parents pay a lot of attention to them. That means 30 percent felt their parents don't pay enough attention to them. As mentioned earlier, our second priority is family. This is second only to our relationship with Jesus. The family should be more important and a higher priority than the job or ministry in the life of a parent. Our first ministry priority is the home.

I learned a long time ago the difference between the "cost" of an item and the "value" of it. A certain item can cost a lot of money, but it may not hold much value. On the flip side, some things that carry small price tags can hold an enormous amount of worth. Investing money in church youth ministry can cost a lot, but its value is immeasurable. The value of a parent spending time with a young person is even more of a treasure. It is an investment that will help determine just how much impact they will have in the lives of their children.

FREEDOM OF EXPRESSION

Keith Olson, in his book *Counseling Teenagers*, identifies three basic needs of teenagers: self-identity, healthy sexuality, and developing primal convictions. Primal convictions could be described as developing one's own value or faith system. My definition is "getting your own Jesus" with an emphasis on individuals finding out the truth about Jesus' person and work. This need is vital in the life of a teenager.

When they are younger, children tend to adopt the worldviews of those around them; but reaching a truly mature faith involves allowing teenagers to ask questions and come to conclusions for themselves. This includes questioning ideas and principles of life that may have been taught by the pastor, youth minister, or other significant adult. The process can be painful for both the student and the adults, but the end result is a student who knows his or her belief is based on personal decision, not assumption.

As parents, we want the "best" for our children. One of the items on the list of "best" things could be allowing them to express themselves. I would be totally remiss if I did not draw a line in the sand and affirm the necessity of drawing appropriate boundaries. But teenagers can learn to express themselves without crossing those lines.

The NSYR research reveals that 81 percent of teenagers believe their parents give them the right amount of room to express their views. This process must involve teaching our children how to think critically. Since God provides security during growth and welcomes honest questions, allowing our children room to think and to question can bring glory to Him. Let me illustrate.

The process of a caterpillar becoming a butterfly is known as *metamorphosis*. While this process of transformation is taking place, the caterpillar is surrounded by a protective cocoon. A person might think he is helping the process by enabling the struggling butterfly to break free before the end of the process, but that's not the case. The butterfly grows stronger by beating its wings against the cocoon walls and fighting to get out. That is the only way flying and survival are possible. If the butterfly breaks free too early, death is a certainty.

As a parent, I must help my child beat their thoughts against the wall of God's Word. My willingness to encourage and allow this process teaches my child a trust in a God who is personal. I am modeling trust and reliability in my God for my child.

Are you feeling uncomfortable at this point? Please stand in line behind me and many other parents. The tendency is for me to "fix" this problem. I do not want my child to struggle in life, certainly not in the area of God's truth. The more space we give our children to struggle with finding "their Jesus," though, the stronger foundation we have laid for them to grow into mature Christian adults. Give them room to strengthen their wings of critical thought about the timeless, unchanging truths of the gospel.

RELIGIOUS CONVERSATION

What do parents and teenagers talk about? The list of subjects might include events at school, relationships, calendar issues, and chit-chat. Apparently, religious or spiritual subjects are not extremely prevalent.

According to the NSYR, 37 percent of the time families never or only a few times a year talk about religion. Even on the high end, only 45 percent of families talk about religion from every day to once a week.

Some topics of conversation can be difficult for a parent and student to broach. The NSYR research found that 54 percent of teenagers sometimes, rarely, or never talked with their father about personal subjects. The research discovered that 44 percent of teenagers sometimes, rarely, or never talked with their mom about personal subjects. Teenagers (43 percent) stated it was fairly or very easy to talk with Mom about sensitive subjects. Compare this with 26 percent who stated it was fairly or very easy to talk with Dad about sensitive subjects.

As mentioned earlier in the book, God commanded the Israelites to take parenting seriously (Deut. 6:6-9). They were called to talk with their children and to answer important spiritual questions. The parents (especially the fathers) in Jewish culture certainly obeyed this command of God. Could this be a statistical and biblical reminder to parents concerning the need to speak about spiritual things on a daily basis? Could it be this practice needs to become a lifestyle displayed in the home from birth?

I have lived in several places in Florida during my life. As you know, a large quantity of citrus fruit is produced in this state. I discovered an interesting truth about oranges. If I cut an orange open, orange juice comes out! I know that may seem to go without saying, but think about this principle as you read Deuteronomy 6 again. What are we pouring into our children as parents? If spiritual things are a natural part of our lives, our children will see the example we portray. But if we only talk about spiritual things once a month (or less), our expectation level concerning spiritual fruit should not be very high.

CONCLUSION

Teenagers are emerging leaders. They deserve our best efforts in developing the kind of adult leadership that can truly influence their lives. The Lone Ranger had Tonto. Batman had Robin. The list could go on, but you get the idea.

Student ministers need adults other than themselves to invest in the lives of teenagers. Multiply your ministry. Better yet, multiply the kingdom of God! You signed up for this tour of duty because you wanted to see God do marvelous things—just as He did in your life. Parents of teenagers and adult leadership are essential if you are to complete your mission. Be real and multiply yourself through others.

ENDNOTES

1. Wayne Rice, *New Directions for Youth Ministry* (Group, Loveland, CO, 1998), 68.

2. Josh McDowell, "Personal Notes on Parenting" *(www.josh.org/Notes/notes.asp)*, 89. Original source: A study done by Shepherd Enoch Pratt Health System titled "The Classroom Avenger."

3. White House Conference on Teenagers: Raising Responsible and Resourceful Youth, "Teens and Their Parents in the 21st Century: An Examination of Trends in Teen Behavior and the Role of Parental Involvement, May 2, 2000, Report by the Council of Economic Advisors," 2.

4. Josh McDowell, "Personal Notes on Parenting" *(www.josh.org/Notes/notes.asp)*, 124. Original source: The Global Strategy Group Of New York City family survey for YMCA of the USA. The Interviews were conducted between March 19 and April 1, 1999.

5. White House Conference on Teenagers: Raising Responsible and Resourceful Youth, "Teens and Their Parents in the 21st Century: An Examination of Trends in Teen Behavior and the Role of Parental Involvement, May 2, 2000, Report by the Council of Economic Advisors," 18.

6. Josh McDowell, Speech presented at Metro Youth Ministers Conference, Destin, FL., 20 April 2004.

7 Ibid.

8. H. Wesley Perkins, "Parental Religion and Alcohol Use Problems as Intergenerational Predictors of Problem Drinking among College Youth." *Journal for the Scientific Study of Religion*, 1987, 26:340-357.

9. Josh McDowell, Speech at Metro Youth Ministers Conference, Destin, FL, 20 April 2004.

10. Ibid.

CHAPTER SIX

Impacting Teenagers at Home

THE RESEARCH

Wesley Black

PARENTING TEENAGERS IS AN AWESOME TASK. It can have wonderful rewards, but it often poses a challenge to parents, especially in the areas of faith, morality, and purity of life. What makes it difficult is the confusing picture of teenagers and their world. Parents get mixed messages about the status of teenage culture, what kind of activities they engage in, how they really behave, and what they believe. It becomes even more muddled in determining the role of faith in their lives and how this affects their daily experiences. Finally, how should parents approach the way they raise their teenage sons and daughters in order to ensure the greatest impact for the kingdom of God?

77

We'll take a quick look at the latest research and what it has to say about the situation in Christian homes.

The Status of Homes with Teenagers

POSITIVE SIGNS

There are some very positive signs for teenagers and their parents. The latest research offers some promising glimpses into the lives of teenagers that will be especially interesting to parents.

1. *Faith and Prayer.* Faith is important in the lives of Southern Baptist teenagers. More than seven out of ten (71 percent) say faith is very or extremely important in shaping how they live their daily lives. Eighty percent say they have made a personal commitment to live life for God.

One interesting point from this study is the connection between relationships with adults and strong faith. Those teenagers who say religious faith is extremely or very important in their day-to-day choices tend to have three to five adults to whom they can turn to in matters of spirituality and faith. But youth who say faith plays a less important role tend to have only one or two adults (or fewer) to help them face matters of spirituality and faith. This speaks volumes to parents and other adults working with teenagers in churches.

Prayer also is important to teenagers. Two-thirds of Southern Baptist teens have an active prayer life in which they pray alone at least a few times a week. More than half of the Southern Baptist teenagers in the NSYR (56 percent) prayed with their parents in the last year.

2. *Witnessing.* At home, six out of ten (61 percent) Southern Baptist teenagers say their families talk about God, the Bible, prayer, or other spiritual things together once a week or more. This is strikingly different from the experiences of teenagers who are not affiliated with any faith or denomination. In the homes of unaffiliated teenagers, only 16 percent say their families talk about God, the Scriptures, prayer, or other religious or spiritual things together once a week or more.

3. *Views of Church.* For the most part, Southern Baptist teenagers and parents both feel good about their church. Less than one in ten (9 percent) Southern Baptist teenagers say, "Church is usually boring." Two-thirds of Southern Baptist parents of teenagers say their church is very or extremely helpful in raising teens, and 80 percent of them say that ministry to teens is a very important priority in their church.

Nearly all Southern Baptist teens (90 percent) say they would go to the same church if it were totally up to them to choose. Could it be that families with teens choose a church with these positive traits because they have teenagers in their families?

4. *Moral/Risky Behaviors.* Despite some common misperceptions, there are marked differences between faithful Christian youth and those with no religious affiliation. For example, in response to these statements:
   - "People should wait to have sex until they are married," nearly two-thirds of Southern Baptist teenagers (66 percent) said yes.
   - "Drink alcohol a few times a month or more," only 9 percent of the Southern Baptist teenagers said they do this.
   - It is OK to have sex if they are "emotionally ready for it," only 3 percent of the faithful Christian teens accept this view.

5. *Moral Reasoning.* This is an area that should be great news to Christian parents. When it comes to morals and honesty, the difference between Christian and non-Christian teenagers is as clear as day.

Overall, faithful Christian teenagers are not as likely to see morals as relative as their nonreligious peers. In response to a question about how they would decide what to do if they were unsure what was right or wrong in a situation, possible responses and percentages are:

- "Do what would help them get ahead" (only 1 percent of Devoted students versus 16 percent of Disengaged students).
- "Do whatever would make them feel happy" (only 6 percent of Devoted students versus 40 percent of Disengaged students).

They could have also selected two other options: (1) to choose to follow the advice of parents, teachers, or other adult authorities; or (2) to do what God or the Scriptures say is right.

In addition, two areas stand out as differences for faithful Christian teens and their nonreligious peers: lying to parents and cheating at school. Devoted teens are four times less likely to lie to their parents than Disengaged teens, and more than twice as many Devoted teens than Disengaged teens say they never lie to their parents. Also faithful Christian teens are significantly less likely to cheat at school and do things they hope their parents never find out about.

NEGATIVE SIGNS

While parents can rejoice in these positive signs, they must not forget there are some negative signs.

1. *Drop in Church Attendance Among Older Teens.* The dropout rate in church attendance (at least 2-3 times per month) for Southern Baptist teens between ages 13-15 and ages 16-27 is highest of all groups in the study. For younger teenagers (ages 13-15), 71 percent say they attend at least 2-3 times per month. But among older teenagers (ages 16-17), that percentage drops to 57 percent. Among unaffiliated (nonreligious) teens, this percentage in church attendance only drops from 15 percent to 14 percent.

2. *Faith in Daily Life.* Take a look at how teenagers responded to the belief that "Faith is very or extremely important in shaping how they live

daily life." For Southern Baptist teens, 75 percent of students ages 13-15 affirm that statement. For those in the 16-17 range, however, the number dives to 67 percent. In contrast, the importance of faith among students who claim no religious affiliation actually grows from 16 percent to 31 percent. This represents the largest increase among all between younger and older teenagers.

3. *Moral/Risky Behaviors.* Some troubling signs for parents of Southern Baptist teens appear in the areas of cheating and lying. *Wait a minute,* you might be thinking, *isn't this one of the strengths mentioned above?* Yes, but there are a couple of points that parents should not miss.

In response to the category, "Cheated in school last year," 58 percent of Southern Baptist teenagers said yes. This percentage equals the 58 percent of unaffiliated teenagers who also confessed to cheating during the past year. Among all teenagers, 62 percent said they cheated in school last year.

In response to the category, "Lied to parents fairly or very often in last year," nearly one in ten (9 percent) of Southern Baptist teenagers agreed. This compares with unaffiliated teenagers who scored only slightly higher (11 percent) and all teenagers scoring at 10 percent.

While these are not startling figures, they should be noted. Parents need to be diligent in helping their teenagers learn to be honest and forthright in their words and actions, at home and in school.

The World of Teenagers

Parents need to be aware of the ways teenagers talk about faith. In a very real way, contemporary adolescents assume a position of politeness and civility when discussing religion, what might be described as a careful and ambiguous inclusiveness. In other words, they do all they can to avoid offending anyone. They are careful to not say the word *Jesus* but will use words like *God* or *higher power.* American teenagers are trained to use correct, ambiguous language. As a result, they are incredibly inarticulate in putting their faith into words.[1]

There is an old story about a group of youngsters in Sunday School. During the class, the teacher was trying to make a point by introducing an object lesson. "What is brown and furry, climbs in trees, and eats nuts?" The students looked puzzled and hesitated to answer. Finally the teacher called on one of the students to answer the question. He looked around the group and finally said, "I know the answer is supposed to be 'Jesus,' but it sure sounds like a squirrel."

Parents and others who work with teenagers in church know that a nagging problem is cutting through the "Sunday School" answers to more realistic, thoughtful responses. Too often, teenagers will just throw out whatever comments they suspect the adult wants.

The Impact of Faith

Parents have some encouraging news about the differences found in the lives of faithful Christian teens. Does following Christ make a difference in adolescent behaviors, rebellion, and unhealthy lifestyles? Some would point to statistics showing there is really no difference between Christians and unbelievers, but the latest study reveals a different picture.

When the lifestyles of these teenagers are compared, there are marked differences between faithful Christian teenagers and their unchurched peers when it comes to risky behaviors and getting into trouble. For example, faithful Christian teens are much less likely to smoke cigarettes, drink alcohol regularly, get drunk, cut classes, be expelled from school, or earn poor grades. In addition, faithful Christian teens are more likely to avoid smoking marijuana. The icing on the cake is that Christian teens are much less likely to be rebellious or to have a bad temper.

These are not just minor differences. In research terms, there are statistically significant differences in most categories between faithful Christian teens and nonreligious teens. This even holds true when other factors such as gender, age, race, region of residence, parental marital status, parents' education, and family income are taken into consideration. Living a faithful life of following Christ makes a difference!

The Impact of the Home

Parents have some important information to consider in terms of the sources of attitudes and behaviors of their teens. While a picture of teenagers dropping out of church in record numbers, rebelling against the faith of parents, and rejecting the Christian heritage of their families has been painted in the past, the research numbers indicate that this is just not the case. The National Study of Youth and Religion found that, "The vast majority of U.S. teens are not alienated or rebellious when it comes to religious involvement. Most are quite content to follow their parents' footsteps" (260).

Teenagers seem to be very similar to their parents in matters of their faith. In his research, Smith found that, "The vast majority are happy simply to accept the one religion in which they were raised. And those with dual-religion parents normally either embrace one, try to pay respect to both, or decide they are not interested in any religion" (260).

It may be easier for parents to point fingers toward outside influences for the ways their teenagers think and act, but the evidence clearly shows that "the single most important social influence on the religious and spiritual lives of adolescents is their parents" (261). Other family members, church youth workers, teachers, coaches, and other adult mentors can have influences, too; but parents seem to be the greatest factor in the religious and spiritual lives of their sons and daughters.

The bottom line is that the spiritual lives of teenagers will turn out to be very much like the spiritual lives of their parents.

Church leaders should note this finding. Congregations that provide the best in programs, opportunities, and relationships for teenagers will have the best track record of holding and challenging teenagers. Churches that give priority to ministry with teenagers and their parents seem much more likely to appeal to teenagers and their families and to foster religious and spiritual maturity in their youth ministries (261).

Response to These Issues

While some parents may throw up their hands ready to surrender when their child reaches the teenage years, this research clearly indicates that is the wrong choice. At least three realities emerge from this study:

1. *Teenagers are eminently teachable.* Both parents and teens desire good communication. Often we hear things like, "Teenagers are so different today, I just don't understand them. We're so far apart that I don't think we can even communicate." The opposite is closer to the truth. Teenagers want to talk to their parents. Parents want to talk to their teenagers. Both could use some help with listening skills, but the desire to communicate is there.

   Parents can help by being more sensitive to "teachable moments." Every situation does not require a lengthy lecture to make an important point. Being available when the teenager wants to discuss something is the most critical step in good parent-teen communication.

Parents cannot ignore the critical task of modeling faith for their teenagers. Smith says, "The best way to get most teenagers more involved in and serious about their faith communities is to get their parents more involved in and serious about their faith communities" (267).

2. *Teenagers desperately need teaching.* When it comes to many things in life, parents take a direct approach to guiding and teaching their teenagers. Most parents do not give their teenagers a choice of whether to attend school or not, and many parents encourage their sons and daughters to be involved in sports and extracurricular activities.

Many parents are very directive when it comes to displaying values such as honesty, hard work, school achievement, and fair play. But these parents suddenly get spineless when it comes to matters of faith. The most recent research clearly encourages parents to be more intentional in communicating the things of God to their teenagers.

3. *Teenagers need teaching approaches that are intentional and directive.* Parents are often intimidated by the growing vocabulary of teenagers. I'm not talking about the teenage slang of the day here. I'm talking about the way complex school subjects can be overwhelming for parents who may not be up on the latest content of English literature, calculus, physics, and economics. Some parents back off trying to teach their teenagers anything because they're afraid of appearing ignorant or out of touch. Match this with teenagers' growing sense of independence and the way some teenagers become hypercritical of their parents, and you have a giant obstacle to communication.

Teenagers are incredibly inarticulate about how to express their faith, their religious beliefs and practices, and its meaning in their lives. Parents should remember that their sons and daughters are putting forth a lot of effort to appear grown-up and independent. The tendency may be to back off and let their teenage sons or daughters just decide for themselves about matters of faith. These parents are missing out on one of the major biblical tasks of parenting: bringing them up *"in the training and instruction of the Lord"* (Eph. 6:4, NIV).

Finally, churches have the obligation of integrating parents into the youth ministry rather than ignoring or sidestepping them. This latest study shows clearly that, "Our findings suggest that overall youth ministry would probably best be pursued in a larger context of family ministry, that parents should be viewed as indispensable partners in the religious formation of youth" (267).

Parenting Approaches

Parents have had to deal with mixed messages about how to guide their children through the adolescent years. Today's culture often seems to say, "Let them sow their wild oats. When they get out of college, get married, and have some kids, they'll settle down and get back in church."

Too often parents settle for the "life script" that says the teenage and young adult years are a time to set aside serious issues and just "live it up." Adults flippantly say, "They're young and need to explore life. When they get a little older, they'll settle down and get back to God and the things of faith. Now they're just wild and crazy, and it's OK. They'll grow out of it."

These parents eagerly turn loose when their child gets into middle or late adolescence; and they offer no guidance, modeling, or input, especially as it relates to matters of faith and religion. "We'll just let them decide for themselves what they want to do about religion" seems to be a common theme. The research, however, points to a need for parents to remain active in their teenagers' lives and to offer appropriate guidance as those teenagers move into this critical stage of life.

The way we raise our children can have an impact on their spiritual growth and development. In the same way, parenting approaches can have an impact on a child's health, education, and all-around well-being. The way we relate to our teenage sons and daughters can also have an impact on their spiritual maturity.

Parenting Approaches that Weaken Spiritual Impact

There are some parenting missteps that should be avoided if we want to strengthen spiritual instruction and impact for our teenagers. The following outline is taken from *Parenting with Kingdom Purpose* by Ken Hemphill and Richard Ross.[2]

1. *Parenting That Is Non-reflective.* While many parents want to provide the best guidance for their teenagers, they go too far by making every decision, setting down every rule and boundary, and never allowing any input from their son or daughter. "As long as you live in this house, you will abide by my rules" may seem logical to parents, but it does little to help teenagers know how to make decisions for themselves. Parents would do well to include their teenagers in the decision-making process, especially as they grow older. This will help teenagers make decisions on their own when they are apart from their parents.

2. *Poor Sense of Self of the Parent.* One of the biggest problems facing parents is how to help a teenager who is struggling with the same problem the parent faced at that age. This can raise emotions and hurts that the parent never fully resolved. The parent may not feel confident handling the situation and will simply explode with outbursts of anger or harsh restrictions. The teenager never really gets any help with the situation. Instead, he or she learns to avoid ever discussing it again.

3. *Parenting That Provokes Children to Anger.* Ephesians 6:1-4 are favorite verses with many parents, because it directs children to *"obey their parents."* But verse 4 speaks clearly about the parental responsibility to not *"provoke your children to anger"* (NASB). Harsh discipline without loving nurture does not draw anyone closer to God. Children and teenagers learn to follow God from what they observe in their parents' words and directives, their spirits and lifestyles.

4. *Parenting That Imposes No Limits or Structure.* When a child becomes a teenager, the urge toward independence begins to blossom. They have a mind of their own, they want to establish their own boundaries, and they want parents to let them have more freedom. Some parents react by tightening the grip. Others react by turning loose too soon. Either way, the teenager suffers. Teenagers may never tell their parents, but they still desire reasonable boundaries and guidance. Most often, teenagers recognize these as acts of love, although they resist telling their parents they appreciate the loving rules and structures.

5. *Parenting That Imposes Limits and Structure but with Weak Relationships.* Rules and restrictions, without a heart connection between parent and teen, become cold and unloving. Teenagers who live in a home without a loving relationship between them and their parents will look forward to the day they can get away from their cold, disconnected parents, and reject all they stand for. Parents have a responsibility to connect with the hearts of their teenagers, in order to better provide the *"nurture and admonition of the Lord"* (Eph. 6:4, KJV). Without this heart connection, the teenager is vulnerable to others who may be eager to connect with one's son or daughter.

6. *Parenting That Allows the Emotional Tanks of the Children to Stay Empty.* How sad it is for someone to grow up without ever hearing parents say such things as "I love you," "You are going to do great things," and "I appreciate you." Parents may fool themselves into thinking that the teen knows this without the parent ever saying it. However, teenagers desperately need the approval and blessing of their parents. Parents need to offer encouragement as well as correction. Otherwise, the teenager will run dry emotionally and look for approval, love, and encouragement from someone else.

7. *Parenting That Allows Children and Teens to Drift Apart.* Normal teenage development can be a trying time for both parents and teens. Teens desire more time alone, apart from their parents. They will often shut the door to their rooms, not begin conversations, and offer only the shortest answers (grunts and one-syllable words) when parents ask about their day or their plans. Parents may just give up and quit trying to communicate. The result is a home that resembles a hotel more than a family dwelling. This can only hurt the opportunity to strengthen spiritual nurture and growth.

8. *Parenting Approaches That Provide Too Little Time for Parents to Be with Their Children.* Busy lifestyles can erase time that parents and teenagers have for each other. Unless we put some effort into managing the time with our families, it will evaporate. When both parents are busy with jobs and tasks, children are busy with school and organizations, and even church activities calling for more and more hours in

the week, families may be scattered with hectic and overwhelming schedules. Parents may mistake a busy lifestyle as inevitable or even a good choice in raising "well-rounded" teenagers. But it tears down the opportunity for parents and teenagers to build strong, emotional bonds through time spent together. It saps the energy for meaningful discussion and input into the lives of teenagers who desperately need to know their parents still love and cherish them.

Parenting Approaches that Strengthen Spiritual Instruction and Impact

There are also some approaches to parenting that can strengthen spiritual instruction and impact.

1. *Parenting That Makes Parents and Children Mutually Accountable.* Many teenagers are willing and eager to commit themselves to purity and boldness in their faith. Sadly, some parents may hesitate to live up to these same standards. There are large numbers of teenagers willing to take the True Love Waits® pledge of sexual purity, but their single and divorced mom or dad hesitates to do the same. There are teenagers struggling to stay sober and off drugs while their parents indulge in alcohol and drugs. This sad lack of accountability can only damage the relationship and the model of faith shared by parents and teens.

Words alone cannot adequately communicate the highest calling in faith. It requires the day-to-day modeling of a lifestyle of faithfulness and commitment. Parents who do the best job of nurturing the faith of their teenagers are the ones who are willing to be open and accountable for the same standards they want to see in the lives of their sons and daughters.

2. *Parenting That Places Reasonable Limits and Structure Around Children and Teenagers.* Some of the most confused teenagers I have ever ministered with are those with no limits. What may seem to be every adolescent's dream (life without any real limits) turns out to be a nightmare. Teenagers have an emotional need for limits that are fair and reasonable. Sure, they may push against the limits and whine about the restrictions, but they still have an often unspoken need for boundaries. Parents will do well to talk with their teens, include them in the bound-

ary-setting process, be willing to explain their thinking processes, and establish reasonable limits and structure for their teenagers.

3. *Parenting That Allows Children and Teenagers to Experience Consequences When They Disobey.* During most of the infant, kindergarten, and childhood years, parents exert a lot of time and energy protecting their children from bad things. They pull hands away from fires and dangerous tools; they stop risky activities; they refuse to allow the child to be involved in dangerous situations; and on and on. But as children move into the teenage and young adult years, they must assume more of the responsibility for their own choices. Parents who continue to rescue their teenagers from every bad situation deprive their sons and daughters of the chance to learn valuable lessons—taking responsibility for and living with the consequences of their own actions and choices.

4. *Parenting That Places the Needs of Children Above the Needs of Parents.* Selfishness is not the sole property of adolescence. Some parents have an abundance of self-centeredness, especially when it comes to making decisions that affect the whole family. Wise fathers consider the needs of their children (emotional, spiritual, relational, and physical) before taking a new job or responsibility. Mothers who consider the needs of their children before taking on new activities and responsibilities will reap years of benefit in their spiritual growth and nurture.

5. *Parenting That Is Authoritative.* A bit of clarification might be helpful here. Most parents may know that the authoritarian parenting style is like the drill sergeant commanding the recruits. Every decision about time, clothing, activities, going to bed, waking up, language, friendships, and so forth, demands immediate, unquestioning obedience.

But what about the authoritative parenting style? In this more effective approach, the parent still retains the final say, while allowing the teenager, as he or she grows older, to have more say in establishing guidelines and boundaries. It is all done with a spirit of love and nurture, acting more in a coaching, guiding way rather than a harsh, demanding way. The parent sees himself or herself as one who guides the teenager in how to make decisions and set boundaries rather than setting all the boundaries and making all the rules for the teenager.

This style of parenting results in a young adult who can function within high standards and boundaries regardless of whether the parent is around or not.

A Concluding Thought

Youth leaders have some things to relish from the latest research on the spiritual formation of Christian teenagers. Yet there are some flags that should catch leaders' attention.

Parenting teenagers is not a job for the weak of heart, but it is a job that can reap a lifetime of joy and satisfaction if approached with the strength that only comes from God. The way we relate to our sons and daughters today can place their hands as close as possible to the hand of God. In contrast, we can choose to ignore the loving spirit of God's hand in our homes and face a life of anxiety and hurt. It really is in God's hands.

THE IMPLICATIONS

Phil Briggs

One of the advantages of staying in student ministry for the long term is watching roles and responses change. Student ministry in the 21st century is more relational than programmatic, and working with parents of teenagers has been one of the greatest adjustments.

Church Leaders Impacting Parents

Even though student ministry professors and leaders have been encouraging parent ministry and impact for more than 25 years, some church leaders are still new to the concept. This is partly due to the age of the ministers who may be faced with impacting parents twice their age. They may be intimidated by adults in the stressful parenting role of guiding adolescents.

If student ministers are to impact the lives of teenagers in middle and high school, they must place a greater degree of emphasis on the primary care givers of teenagers—the parents. Some younger ministers, including pastors, are still in the throes of emancipating themselves from their own parents. If this is the case, wrapping their minds around the needs of parents of any age may be stressful. Even so, they must grow quickly in order to minister effectively.

Setting the Stage for Parent Impact

Student ministers must build bridges to parents with wise and careful relationships. Love, integrity, and good administration all are important ingredients to the parent ministry recipe.

LOVE THEIR KIDS

There are ways to get the parents' ear and their cooperation. One true avenue to the hearts of parents is through their children, and this is best accomplished by showing them how much you love their teens. Parents seldom resent people who offer genuine love, appreciation, and assistance. Some parents are so close to their children they miss seeing the potential of their offspring. By discovering and developing their teenagers' gifts and abilities, ministers and other significant adults can offer adolescents a platform for putting those skills into practice.

MINISTER WITH INTEGRITY

A student minister must be dependable and maintain his or her own personal integrity. Here lies one of the trickiest trails to travel for young student ministers. Building one's integrity begins with a healthy maturation process where actual behavior corresponds positively with the type of behavior expected of one who guides and mentors teenagers. Sometimes the youthful student minister perceives that he or she must behave with the youthful enthusiasm and abandon displayed by many teenagers. While student ministers should be able to identify with their teenagers, though, they certainly do not need to become identical to them. Parents tend to interpret these characteristics as immature; and, as a result, they may resist giving loyalty and authority to the minister.

SHOW GOOD ADMINISTRATIVE SKILLS

This integrity construction also demands good planning and administrative procedures for student events. For example, a student minister's failure to plan a trip well with regard to time and expense can undercut integrity. Likewise, having the bus arrive past the announced time can mean more than simply a group of irritated parents. It also might mean that the minister's integrity and dependability are compromised in the eyes of those parents. Ministers will gain the respect and the loyalty of parents when there is adequate planning and execution of details.

Evangelizing and Discipling Parents of Teenagers

The National Study of Youth and Religion has made clear that most teenagers will be very similar to their parents in matters of faith. When parents are lost, this is a critical issue.

The ministers' strategy should include expending greater energy in evangelism toward parents of teenagers. Nothing promotes the spiritual transformation of the family like the conversion of a parent, so this should be an intentional objective.

Alert student ministers are aware that many parents seldom relate to the church. Even though they send or encourage their teenagers to be in student ministries, they have no personal involvement. Consequently, many of these uninvolved parents are nonbelievers who should be reached.

The Great Commission implores the church to make disciples, and this includes taking the time to evangelize parents. In fact, we are not just called to evangelize them, but also to nurture them in discipleship. Parents can't lead children where they themselves have not been. All pastoral and administrative energies should focus on this task. Research suggests that assisting parents in becoming spiritually alive will almost always result in teenagers becoming spiritually alive.

Equipping Parents to Disciple Their Children

Ministry must focus on the family and reinforce the parents' role. To emphasize this vital responsibility of the parents, we need to take a closer look at Deuteronomy 6:4-9. In verse 7, God tells Israel that they must, *"teach (God's laws) diligently unto thy children, and shalt talk of them when thou sittest in thine house, and when thou walkest by the way, and when thou liest down, and when thou risest up"* (KJV).

The word *diligently* is a Hebrew word picturing the sharpening of a knife or tool in both directions. The passage also means that parents should live out their faith and be spiritually vibrant kingdom builders. Many parents have no idea of how to accomplish this task. So church ministers must equip parents to become the spiritual leaders of their children.

Part of that leadership will take place informally. Parents should realize that they are teaching truth as they live out the full counsel of Scripture in front of their children. Parents also can teach truth as they bring up topics of faith in the normal flow of family life.

Informal impact is vital but should not stand alone. The raising of kingdom-focused teenagers also demands more formal times for teaching and spiritual impact.

The National Study of Youth and Religion makes clear:

1. Teenagers are eminently teachable at home.
2. Teenagers desperately need teaching.
3. Teenagers need teaching approaches that are intentional and directive.

Practically speaking, this means church leaders need to:

1. *Lead parents to pray for impact as they teach their children.* Without prayer, their teaching will have limited impact.
2. *Show parents how to teach truth to their children.* Few parents will attempt teaching if they fear failure.
3. *Give parents a plan for teaching truth to their children.* For busy families, gathering two to three times a week may be realistic.
4. *Place in the hands of parents the printed resources they need to teach truth.* Busy parents need help mining the truths from Scripture and planning creative ways to communicate with their children.
5. *Lead parents to plan ways the family can pray together.*

Here are important questions for church leaders to consider.

- How much money does the church spend training volunteers to teach the Bible at church?
- How much money does the church spend training parents to teach the Bible at home?
- How much money does the church spend on curriculum for teaching the Bible at church?
- How much money does the church spend on resources for teaching the Bible in homes?
- Do the ministers consider it their job to have an effective Bible teaching organization at church?
- Do the ministers consider it their job to have effective Bible teaching in homes?

If discipling done by parents is central to the spiritual transformation of children, then equipping parents to become the spiritual leaders of their children is the job of ministers. Judges 2:10 offers believers a stern warning if parents do not fulfill their role: *After that whole generation had been gathered to their fathers, another generation grew up, who knew neither the LORD nor what he had done for Israel* (NIV).

Never before in the history of the church has there been a more crucial time for leaders to train and support parents. Current parents are consumers and are expecting much from the church. When this involves teenagers, they view their needs as critical.

The psalmist offers parents a challenge which is still worthy today.

> [4] *We will not hide them from their children;*
>   *we will tell the next generation*
> *the praiseworthy deeds of the LORD,*
>   *his power, and the wonders he has done.*
> [5] *He decreed statutes for Jacob*
>   *and established the law in Israel,*
> *which he commanded our forefathers*
>   *to teach their children,*
> [6] *so the next generation would know them,*
>   *even the children yet to be born,*
>   *and they in turn would tell their children.*
> [7] *Then they would put their trust in God*
>   *and would not forget his deeds*
>   *but would keep his commands.*
> [8] *They would not be like their forefathers—*
>   *a stubborn and rebellious generation,*
>   *whose hearts were not loyal to God,*
>   *whose spirits were not faithful to him.*
>   Psalm 78:4-8 (NIV)

Honest Questions from Teenagers

Parents would do well to allow their teenagers to make faith and belief their own. Parents whose only response to honest questioning of faith is, "because I said so" may raise teenagers who have no personal, owned faith, much less a faith that can sustain them for a lifetime.

For years I have suggested to parents that they let their children "be wrong for a while" about what they believe. Give them space to ponder and take ownership of their beliefs since faith formation is a very personal process. God does not have any "grandchildren," so our children must make personal commitments of faith and take steps toward transformation over time.

If parents honor all Scriptures as the Word of God and if they live consistent with those Scriptures, most children will resolve their questions and will come to the same convictions as their parents. If parents honor all Scriptures as the Word of God and live with strong heart connections with their children, there is an even greater likelihood that those children will embrace the truthfulness of all Scripture.

Family discussions about faith are woefully absent in most homes. In a recent sabbatical study, I interviewed about 500 college students in 39 states. Only one student indicated that she discussed religion in her home. Little has changed since Merton Strommen's study in 1985, which indicated that only 32 percent of those he interviewed discussed religion at home, yet 97 percent of the respondents were church members.[3]

It is very crucial for parents to give teenagers time to assimilate their belief system. Expecting immediate and exacting compliance with parental beliefs is unrealistic for faith-developing teenagers.

Family Discussion Exercise

As indicated above, few families discuss religious themes at home. Following are some suggested topics and questions to consider for discussion starters in this area:

- God exists as Father, Son, and Holy Spirit.
- Are humans special creatures made in the image of God or simply a recent development in the process of animal evolution?
- Jesus Christ may have been a great ethical teacher, as other men have been in history, but was He the divine Son of God?
- The Bible is the Word of God given to guide humans to grace and salvation.
- Are those who believe God really answers prayers just deceiving themselves?
- It is ridiculous to believe that Jesus Christ could be both human and divine.

- Jesus was born of a virgin.
- The Bible may be an important book of moral teachings, but it was no more inspired by God than were many other such books in the history of man.
- The concept of God is an old superstition that is no longer needed to explain things in the modem era.
- Will Christ really return to the earth some day?
- Most world religions have miracle stories in their traditions; but there is no reason to believe any of them are true, including those found in the Bible.
- God hears all of our prayers.
- God made man in His own image and breathed life into him.
- Historically, we know that Jesus was crucified, died, and was buried, but how do we really know He rose from the dead on the third day?
- Jesus miraculously changed real water into real wine.
- Does God concern Himself with every action of humans?
- Jesus' death on the cross, if it actually occurred, did nothing in and of itself to save the human race.
- The resurrection proves beyond a doubt that Jesus is the Christ or Messiah of God.

Adolescents want to come to grips with the living Word who will help them live today, not just in the future. Where should we begin utilizing the Scriptures effectively in the religious educational process? The Bible must be a valuable text for home use, helping parents guide the way for both family and personal life.

We must develop within parents, teachers, and pastors a basic understanding of the principles of biblical hermeneutics by emphasizing the science of biblical interpretation and the basic principles that must be followed. The goal is not to produce robotic religionists. Instead, we want to nurture strong believers who recognize that one cannot simply "read through" the Scriptures and comprehend them.

Research has affirmed that teens and parents have a deep hunger for purpose and meaning in life. They are looking for something in which they can believe and to which they can give their lives. Christ is at work to satisfy this hunger and does so through Bible study, prayer, worship, and service. In the process the family becomes central. Scripture is filled with evidence that the family holds a key place in Christian education:

- Jesus was born into a family, and Paul's writings are filled with family instructions (Eph. 5:22—6:4; Col. 3:18-21; 2 Tim. 1:5).
- In the Old Testament, the relationship of God to Israel often was couched in family illustrations (Jer. 3;20-22; Ezek. 16:30-32; Hos. 2:19-20; 11:1-4).
- In the early New Testament era, the home and church were practically synonymous in Jewish thought and culture.
- Most religious ceremonies were in the home, and parents were the religious leaders.
- Later the temple was the meeting place.
- It is noteworthy that when the religious meeting places were destroyed, the family survived as did their faith. The home was the primary institution.

The family should not only discuss religion, but have a commitment to serve others. Church leaders can encourage families to turn such common events as a trip to the store into fun events by sharing groceries with the needy in the community. Leaders can transform family vacations into journeys of faith and mission opportunities instead of just a ski trip for parents and teenagers.

Spiritual development in the home must include evangelism (2 Tim. 1:3-5; 1 Cor. 7:10-16). Evangelism can be directed toward a lost family member or lost persons who come under the influence of the family.

Worship is another family function contributing to spiritual development. This differs from church worship and can be tailored to the family needs. It allows every member to be a contributor. Worship can occur, as an example, during nature walks with time set aside for prayers of thanksgiving for God's creation.

Parent Education

Sadly, many parents replicate the flawed practices of their own parents. Parent training is often a midcourse correction in the way they were raised. We can't tell them what to do if we do not train them to do it.

So, student ministers must be parent trainers. This is a challenge especially for the young youth minister who may be single or yet to become a parent. Student ministers don't have to be the experts in training, but they do need to ensure that it gets done.

The minister must earn the right to be heard and to minister to parents by building a trust relationship with the parents. A simple thing such as learning the names of both teenagers and family members can help in building this relationship.

Train Parents to Build Heart Connections

Parents cannot teach truth until the hearts of the parents and of the children have been turned toward each other. The crucial ingredient is time. Warm parent-child relationships can only be developed with time. Quality of time is never as valuable as quantity of time. Parents are to strengthen and rebuild the heart connections that run between the hearts of parents and the hearts of the children.

Thousands of families have found deeper heart connections after experiencing *30 Days, Turning the Hearts of Parents and Teenagers Toward Each Other* by Richard Ross and Gus Reyes (LifeWay®). One parent and one teenager commit to 15-minute, guided conversations at bedtime for 30 days. Each night they break a seal in the resource to discover what they are to say to each other. Some nights there is laughter and some nights there are tears. Every night there is a fresh way to pray for each other. Night after night the bond between the two grows stronger and stronger.

Parents who have lost the heart of a child find it difficult, if not impossible, to teach truth in a way that leads to transformation. That is why experiences such as *30 Days* are so strategic. Until the heart connection is established again, spiritual growth and transformation usually do not begin.

No technique for raising children can be truly successful unless the parent is flexible, courageous, and open to self-examination. Establishing a positive parent-child relationship requires the parent change as necessary, as well as the child.

Support or Share Groups

The church and its parent trainers can help reduce anxiety in the family. The trainer can help parents deal with their feelings in healthy ways through parent share groups. Nothing helps like the discovery that they are not alone in this experience.

Often parents sweat the little things when the focus should be on the big picture. For example, one can get so sidetracked by the daily encounters that relations with the whole family are never checked. Does the parent react to all the children in the same manner or only over-react to a growing, changing adolescent? Parents are not powerless to provide guidance and leadership to their children.

Training in Communication

Probably one of the most important ingredients in the mix of working together as a family is the art of communication. Most teenagers tend to reduce their talking time to parents. Why? Among the reasons they give are:

- It is not "cool"; with peers, yes, but not with parents.
- Talking with parents is a sign of dependence; they want to experience independence.
- Parents and teens live in different worlds and social sectors; there are not always things to talk about.
- Parents tend to pry and ask dumb questions.
- If teens don't talk, they feel that they are in control of the situation and which, strangely, makes them feel better about the situation.

Even though teenagers do seem to communicate less in adolescence, they still desire some level of communication. The National Study of Youth and Religion—as well as many other major studies—confirm that teenagers want to stay connected to parents. Because contemporary parents tend to become preoccupied with their own adult lives, they are offering less communication to their teenagers than the teenagers desire. Parents who assume their children no longer want to talk to them need to know that this is not the case.

Recently, my young grandson brought a video game while spending the day with me. It was a home-run derby baseball game, and he wanted me to play it with him. He went first and on nearly every pitch he put the ball over the fence. When it was my turn, I thought it would be a piece of cake. After all, back in my college days, I was a varsity letterman and a good hitter. Well, was I surprised! I never even hit one pitch, much less put it out of the park. What was the deal? Timing!

Parent trainers must help parents work on timing. Sometimes parents pass on good advice, but it comes at the wrong time. Perhaps the best stance a parent can take is to cut back on talking to their children and invest some time listening.

Wise parents acknowledge the flash points in family communication and recognize that growing teenagers learn while they are talking. Parents who disconnect the interchange with their child thwart development of good communication. This process is magnified in the findings that show that teenagers need approaches to teaching that are intentional and directive.

By contrast, an unwise parent limits the number of verbal exchanges with their children. Since relating to and communication with teenagers is so necessary in the growing family, it's smart to know where tension points may occur. Parents should learn the areas of conflict, such as beliefs and values, home and family, school, and social life. If parents fail to show respect for the teenager, especially in highly-charged emotional times, hurtful words can be exchanged. When talking with teenagers, parents need to keep Ephesians 4:29 near the front of their memories:

Do not let any unwholesome talk come out of your mouths, but only what is helpful for building others up according to their needs, that it may benefit those who listen (NIV).

To avoid the pitfalls in communication, parents can share control through "thinking words." "Thinking words" is the use of gentle words to help teenagers, not the parent, make choices and determine the outcome. By using thinking words, we tell teenagers what we will allow, what we will do, and what we will accept.

Some principles for communication are:

- *Restrict talking to friendly conversation and use a respectful tone of voice.* To influence the child, the parent must learn to curb criticism and talk in a positive vein. The tone of voice should convey respect and value for the child as a person.
- *Be both firm and kind.* When the parent decides on a course of action, he must not vacillate; he must remember to be friendly, non-judgmental and matter-of-fact when applying a consequence.

- *Keep your control.* Children often try to gain control by demanding special attention. Responding with anger rarely accomplishes anything. Try to remain calm, matter-of-fact, and capable of planning an effective course of action.
- *Utilize encouragement.* The parent can encourage the child by recognizing effort and contribution, as well as accomplishment. By demonstrating that he or she understands how the teenager feels when things aren't going well, encouragement can be given even if the child is not entirely successful.
- *Have courage.* While the parent is restraining himself or herself and the teenager, parents may have to try out new methods several times. Changing behavior requires practice and patience. When new approaches fail, parents should not despair. Instead, they should stop and analyze their feelings and actions, then learn how to proceed differently next time.

Training in Discipline

Parents need specific training in how to discipline their teenagers, especially when their children become too big to spank. Church parents know biblical discipline is part of raising kingdom children, but they may not know how to approach discipline during the teenage years.

Many parents respond to disobedience with emotional outbursts or long lectures. Usually those are weak responses that carry limited impact. Shouting tends to hinder behavior change in the long-term, and it usually weakens the heart connection between parent and child. Parents who want kingdom teenagers to emerge from their homes will stop using emotional outbursts as their primary response to bad behavior.

Parents need instruction in using natural and logical consequences as a part of discipline. A misbehaving teenager seldom benefits from punishment that is unrelated to the disobedience. Instead, the parent must allow the teenager to experience reality's lessons through the use of logical and natural consequences.

Wise parents allow the teenager to experience a reasonable amount of pain or inconvenience when he behaves irresponsibly. By not stepping in to rescue a child from the consequence of disobedience, parents are using natural consequences as part of discipline.

But sometimes natural consequences are not strong enough or quick enough. In those instances, parents must create logical consequences—unpleasant consequences orchestrated by the parents, but still connected in a logical way to the disobedience.

Delivery System

About the only way to train parents in their parenting roles and as the primary spiritual leaders in their homes is to assemble them. As noted earlier, a youth minister or other church leader may be the primary trainer of parents. Alternately, the minister may be the driving force behind training, but he or she may bring in other "experts" to stand before parents.

Smaller churches with volunteer or partially-funded youth leaders should consider at least two parent training events per year. In some regions, several churches could combine their resources to provide stronger training and impact on parents. Churches with fully-funded youth ministers should consider monthly gatherings. The summer months and December are problematic, so eight events a year may be more realistic.

Providing eight parent events a year will require staff time, volunteer help, and budget resources. Those who have not read this book may think eight gatherings a year is too many. But the National Study of Youth and Religion, scores of similar studies, and especially the Word of God make it clear that parents are central to the spiritual transformation of teenagers. With that fact as context, it makes perfect sense to move time, energy, and resources in that direction.

Conclusion

It was once said that a parent's version of Proverbs 22:6 should read, "Train up a child in a way he should go—and walk there yourself once in a while." Christian example is where it all comes to rest in parenting.

In a personal interview in 1994, Merton Strommen said that effective parenting includes intentionality on the part of the parent. Parents must deliberately decide to have a healthy Christian family. He contends it must be as conscious as nonfat foods or other dietary decisions, only in the spiritual realm. Foundationally, there is to be the building of intimacy in the family and with God. He declares that parents develop such intimacy when the faith of the parent is evident and growing, when moral codes are communicated, and when the family is engaged

in mission action service. Some keys to remember include:
- Faith in God plays a foundational role in daily family life.
- Religion strengthens the core of the family support system
- Parents are to feel a strong responsibility for passing the faith in positive and meaningful ways.
- Help parents redefine their role in kid's faith. Move them beyond the roles of taxi drivers, cooks, and bottle washers and into the position of faith nurturers.

Teaching parents how to invest in the spiritual resources of their children can produce incalculable rewards. The result not only guides the child toward God, but it also reinforces an attitude of caring and concern toward the needs of those around them. This is why ministers must equip parents in biblical and parenting skills. They must help parents overcome their feelings of inadequacy and empower them to fulfill the primary task God has given them in the home.

ENDNOTES

1. Christian Smith with Melinda Lundquist Denton, *Soul Searching: The Religious and Spiritual Lives of American Teenagers* (Oxford University Press, 2005), 160.

2. Ken Hemphill and Richard Ross, *Parenting with Kingdom Purpose* (Broadman, Nashville, 2005), 55-76.

3. Merton P. Strommen and A. Irene Strommen, *Five Cries of Parents* (Harper & Row, 1985), 134.

CHAPTER SEVEN

Impacting Teenagers at Church

THE RESEARCH

Brian Richardson

DAVE HUNG UP THE PHONE in stunned disbelief. This 44-year-old Sunday School teacher of teenage boys had just received a call telling him two of the boys in his class were arrested for shoplifting. These boys had attended his class for more than a year, made professions of faith in Jesus as their Savior, and outwardly showed all the signs of being committed Christians. Now Dave wondered if the church really had made any impact on the lives of these (or any other) adolescents. Was it worth all the time and effort he put into teaching this class or was it all just a waste of time?

Just how are Southern Baptist churches doing in the spiritual development of our teens? How will those teens turn out? Will they be good citizens, well-adjusted adults, spiritually mature Christians? Or will they rebel against their spiritual roots?

Some writers claim that teenagers today are alienated from traditional churches and that they are dropping out of organized religion as soon as they are able to decide for themselves.[1] The exhaustive research done by the National Study of Youth and Religion suggests that this stereotype has little basis in fact, especially for Southern Baptist teenagers.

This chapter provides the information needed to understand how Southern Baptist teenagers feel about "organized" religion and the impact it is having on their lives. The implications of this research enable us to minister more effectively to the spiritual needs of today's teens.

How Southern Baptist Teenagers View the Church

The NSYR research team has concluded that in the lives of American adolescents "religion clearly operates in a social-structurally weak position, competing for time, energy, and attention and often losing against other more dominant demands and commitments—particularly against school, sports, television, and other electronic media."[2] The question for us is, "Is this also true for Southern Baptist teenagers?"

Prior studies concluded that only a minority of adolescents (40 percent) desire to be actively involved in a local church.[3] Some claim that teenagers today have more of a spiritual experience and sense of community when they participate in faith groups on the Internet than in the churches they attend. This stereotype has led many to conclude that teenagers are alienated from organized religion.

View of the Church by SBC Teenagers

The study by Smith and his colleagues, however, discovered that teenagers express a strong affiliation to their churches, and this affiliation was stronger for Southern Baptist teenagers than for those from other religious groups. (See Table 4.) Almost 90 percent of Southern Baptist teenagers would go to the same church if the choice were left up to them and more than 61 percent would attend on a regular basis.

Currently about 51 percent of Southern Baptist teens attend both Sunday School and church almost every week. According to this research, these youth seem to have found something fulfilling in their churches.

TABLE 4. VIEWS OF CHURCH (AMONG THOSE WHO ATTEND)

	Would Go to the Same Church if It Were Totally Up to Teen (percentages)
Southern Baptist Convention	90
Conservative Protestant	88
Mainline Protestant	84
Black Protestant	87
All Protestants	87
Catholic	78
Unaffiliated	74
All Teenagers	84

Source: National Study of Youth and Religion, 2002-3.

Southern Baptist teenagers have a stronger affiliation for their church than teenagers from other denominations. We need to know, however, if there is a growth in youth disaffection toward the church over the last decade. Maybe the overall view of teenagers today about organized religion is positive, but is there a downward trend? According to Smith, evidence from 20 years of surveys conducted as part of the "Monitoring the Future" program shows no such downward trend—in fact relatively little has changed at all.[4] These positive attitudes of teenagers appear to have been quite unwavering for two decades, and differences between teenagers and parental beliefs about religion have actually declined over this period. Because parents have the greatest impact on the religious beliefs of teens, this fact is significant.

Smith used various indicators to determine if American teens were alienated from organized religion. Among these indicators were the following questions: "How closely do your ideas agree with your parents' about religion?" and "If you have at least an average income in the future, how likely is it that you will contribute money to church or religious organizations?" These questions were designed to determine both a general sense of spirituality and specific attitudes toward the "established" religion from which teenagers are often said to be alienated.

1. *"How closely do your ideas agree with your parents' about religion?"*
   Among Southern Baptist teenagers, more than 70 percent say their religious beliefs are similar or very similar to those of their mothers, with only four percent saying their beliefs are very different from the views held by their mothers. The impact of fathers on the religious beliefs of teenagers was considerably less, with only 58 percent saying they held religious beliefs similar or very similar to those of their fathers. The percentage that held religious beliefs very different from their fathers, however, was also just four percent.

   The impact that parents, especially mothers, have on the attitudes of teenagers toward organized religion is profound and indicates that Southern Baptist teens are not alienated from organized religion. The research shows the importance of helping parents share their faith with their children and to live that faith as an example before them.

2. *If you have at least an average income in the future, how likely is it that you will contribute money to church or religious organizations?*
   When Southern Baptist teens were asked if they had given $20 or more to their church, 52 percent said no, but almost 48 percent said yes. Because teens control so much money today and because where

they spend or give their money is an indication of their values, more than half of our teenagers are voting against the church by their unwillingness to support financially what they claim to believe.

The percentage of Southern Baptist teens who support the church, however, is similar to the percentage who attend regularly. Perhaps the number that support the church will increase as we find ways to get more Southern Baptist teenagers to attend regularly.

Relationships are important to teens, and the warmth that Southern Baptist teenagers experience within their churches may explain the positive feelings about their church. When asked if they felt welcome at their church, 81 percent said they usually felt welcome, with only 2.5 percent saying they rarely were made to feel welcome.

It is encouraging to learn that some 64 percent of Southern Baptist teenagers found that church stimulates their thinking, while only 9 percent found it boring. The implication is that teenagers who attend church find it stimulating and warm—a place to discuss serious issues.

In addition, this study indicates that if leaders can get adolescents to attend church regularly, those adolescents will find that the church can meet their needs with a high level of effectiveness. Since about half of all Southern Baptist teens do not attend church on a regular basis, the task remains to attract them to the ministry of the church.

The Impact of Faith on Life

The data concerning the influence of religion on the lives of teenagers is mixed. Impressively, a majority of teens say that religion is a positive force both in shaping daily life and in making major life decisions.[5]

Unfortunately, a comprehensive analysis of what teenagers mean when they say religion is very important to them reveals that it may not be as positive as initially thought. Apparently, religion is important to teens when it relates to things considered strictly religious (prayer, basic religious beliefs, church attendance, etc.); but it fails to carry the same amount of influence when it comes to areas considered "outside" the church. To make the matter even more poignant, these "outside" areas are where adolescents face challenges every day.

To get a better idea of the impact of religion, interviewers asked teens for specific examples of how religious faith influenced the way they lived. Quite often, the teenagers admitted that they did not see religion influencing their dating relationships, their conduct at school, or even their relationships within their families (140).

One teenager articulated this prominent attitude when he said, "Church makes me learn more about God and Jesus, but that's about it; it doesn't have any effect on my life" (139). Another teen added that, "Praying and reading devotionals and going to church is just something I do. I don't think I've gotten to the how-it-affects-me yet" (159). They see religion's value in how it provides useful guidance and training for becoming good people, which is a key issue among youth (150).

These statistics point out that teenagers tend to compartmentalize their lives. Religion is important, but they do not connect it to their everyday living. As a result, they live in two separate spheres and fail to grasp how one sphere can (or should) interact with the other.

Eighty percent of Southern Baptist teenagers say they have made a personal commitment to live for God, and 72 percent say that commitment determines how they live each day. (See Table 5.) Their responses to lifestyle questions, though, reveal several inconsistencies.

It appears that Southern Baptist teenagers see their faith as useful and valuable when they are at church or when they need God for something. They do not see their faith as truth that transforms their lives (154). This becomes a major concern for youth leaders because Jesus makes it clear that what we believe determines how we live. He said, *You are My friends, if you do what I command you*" (John 15:14, NASB).

TABLE 5. FAITH AND RELIGIOUS EXPERIENCES (PERCENTAGES)

	Faith Is Very or Extremely Important In Shaping How They Live Daily Life	Made a Personal Commitment to Live Your Life for God
Southern Baptist Convention	72	80
Conservative Protestant	67	79
Mainline Protestant	50	60
Black Protestant	73	74
All Protestants	66	73
Catholic	41	41
Unaffiliated	23	27
All Teenagers	51	55

Source: National Study of Youth and Religion, 2002-3.

Other responses support the conclusion that teenagers compartmentalize their lives. When asked if people should wait for sex until married, 34 percent of Southern Baptist teenagers said it was not necessary to wait. Even though 66 percent said people should wait until married to have sex, 41 percent said they would live with a romantic partner without being married. In addition, 21 percent of Southern Baptist teens admit to having oral sex, and 25 percent have had sexual intercourse. These statistics clearly show that the message that our faith should affect our daily behavior is not reaching a large percentage of Southern Baptist teens; or, if it is reaching them, they are choosing to ignore this truth.

On the positive side, this research discovered that the more teens are actively involved with their local church the less likely they are to smoke, drink alcohol, use marijuana, watch R-rated movies, view pornographic Web sites or engage in other morally questionable activities.

Religious practice clearly does influence the lives of teens. We must encourage parents, therefore, to lead their teenagers in becoming involved in the teaching ministry of the local church.

Teenagers Are Teachable at Church

The NSYR discovered that teenagers rate their religious congregations with high marks for teaching them what they want to know about their faith and that very few teens find the church boring. (See Table 6.)

TABLE 6. VIEWS OF CHURCH (AMONG THOSE WHO ATTEND) (PERCENTS)

	Their Church Usually Makes Teen Think About Important Things	Church Is Usually Boring	Their Church Usually Feels Warm and Welcoming to Teen	Church Is a Very Good Place to Talk About Serious Issues
Southern Baptist Convention	64	9	81	57
Conservative Protestant	70	10	80	52
Mainline Protestant	58	16	82	38

Source: National Study of Youth and Religion, 2002-3.

Those who should be best able to judge if the church does a good job of teaching are the teens who attend church the most frequently. In this group, Southern Baptist teenagers were generally positive about their church with 69 percent saying the church helps them think through some important aspects of their faith. Likewise, 57 percent say the church is a good place to talk about serious issues like family problems, alcohol, or troubles at school that affect their lives. They especially are positive about the youth group in their church, which they say provides a good and positive environment for learning about faith and talking about serious life issues.

When teenagers enjoy their youth groups, feel the church is warm and welcoming, and believe the church is a good place to discuss the serious issues of life, a very fertile field for teaching has been created. Very often, however, churches are under considerable pressure to entertain teenagers instead of teaching them the fundamentals of the faith. The limited time most churches have with teenagers each week often causes the entertainment motif to take precedence over solid biblical teaching in the church.

In addition, many laypeople have trouble teaching religion to teenagers. They may not have this problem when it comes to teaching sports, music, or school; but teaching religion intimidates them (267). We need to help adults understand how much our teenagers are looking for spiritually mature adults to teach them the things of God.

Teenagers and Adults at Church

The NSYR discovered that most church-attending teenagers have nonparental adults in their congregations to whom they enjoy talking, from whom they receive encouragement, and with whom they feel comfortable enough to seek advice and help. Those youth who do not have such adult relationships wish they did. Less than two percent of Southern Baptist teenagers said they did not have an adult they could turn to for support while 43 percent had three to five adults they could rely on. In addition, 11 percent of those teenagers had as many as 10 significant adults in their lives.

One young lady, Alyssa, says she enjoys what she calls her "spiritual mother and father" at church. Her story, as recounted by the NSYR researchers, illustrates the important role significant, nonparental adults play in the lives of contemporary teenagers.

"My real dad supports me with money and stuff like that," Alyssa said, "but these are parents that you can actually talk to like friends. They are very helpful, like when I can't go to my dad on certain things 'cause he won't understand it, I go to them. They're very understanding, but at the same time, if you know better and still do something, they'll tell you what's wrong with that and rebuke you. It's very helpful just to have someone like that around. My spiritual mother, . . . she's just a woman of God, she's really cool. Ever since [we met] she's just been counseling me" (114).

Southern Baptist churches are particularly helpful in fostering cross-generational relationship ties that strengthen the religious faith and practices of teenagers. Meaningful and personal adult relationships with students are more important in the effective teaching of those students than new methods or programs.

Southern Baptist teens come to church regularly, enjoy the services and relationships they have there, listen to their ministers and mentoring adults, and believe they are well taught. But where do they go from there? After being exposed to the truths of God's Word, are they able to articulate their faith?

Teenagers Stating Their Beliefs

The in-depth interviews conducted with teenagers in the NSYR demonstrated that the vast majority were unable to articulate their religious beliefs and could not explain how those beliefs connect to the rest of their lives (131). As mentioned in an earlier chapter, when teenagers talked to researchers about "grace," they were usually talking about the television show "Will and Grace," not about God's grace. Likewise, when students mentioned being "justified," they thought about having a valid reason for questionable conduct and not the theological truth of having one's relationship with God made right (167).

Most teenagers know vivid details about the lives of stars in television, movies, music, and sports; but they know almost nothing about the teachings of the Bible or even the life of Jesus.

"Our impression as interviewers was that many teenagers could not articulate matters of faith because they have not been effectively educated in and provided opportunities to practice talking about their faith," wrote NSYR lead researcher Christian Smith (133). The interviewers concluded that the majority of teens in the U.S. would badly fail any test on the basic beliefs of their faith (137).

Southern Baptist teenagers have stronger beliefs in several key doctrines than do most religious teenagers. (See Table 7.) Belief in a particular doctrine does not mean they can articulate that belief; but if they do not believe it, they certainly will not learn to articulate it. What is disturbing about Southern Baptist teens is that 40 percent do not believe in life after death, and 51 percent do not feel very close to God.

TABLE 7. BELIEF IN SELECTED CHRISTIAN DOCTRINES (PERCENTS)

	Definitely Believes in Life After Death	Definitely Believes in Existence of Angels	Definitely Believes in the Possibility of Divine Miracles from God	Believes in Judgment Day	Believes in God	Feel Very or Extremely Close to God
Southern Baptist Convention	60	79	74	88	96	49
Conservative Protestant	62	79	77	88	94	48
Mainline Protestant	51	59	59	63	86	40
Black Protestant	50	76	76	91	97	49
All Protestants	56	73	72	83	93	47
Catholic	45	58	53	67	85	31
Unaffiliated	37	39	35	49	62	18
All Teenagers	49	63	61	71	84	36

Source: National Study of Youth and Religion, 2002-3.

We have already seen that teenagers believe the church does a good job of teaching them about "religious" things. Why then are teenagers so inarticulate about their faith? The major reason seems to be that so much of their time is taken up by school, homework, sports, parties, daily schedules, relationships, television, movies, music, the Internet, and so forth. Once an individual devotes a great of time to these interests and concerns, there is little time left for religion.

Even if they attend church activities on a regular basis, they are not learning even the facts about their faith, perhaps because they are happy with the relationships they have in their local church or are content to believe what their parents believe. They see no reason to worry about learning "all that doctrine." Also many parents communicate to their children the idea that homework and sports take priority over church or youth group attendance.

It is evident that churches need to find effective and creative ways to involve teenagers in more in-depth Bible studies that will give them the opportunity to publicly explain their faith. As noted earlier, youth leaders also should enlist the support of families in making Bible knowledge and personal application priorities in the lives of teenagers.

Teenagers View Religion in a Benignly Positive Light

Most American teenagers do not have what we would consider militant views about religion. Teenagers who consider themselves religious are glad that religion is a part of their lives because it provides them with a sense of security and happiness without adding very much interference to their lifestyles. True to the culture of tolerant attitudes, teenagers who consider themselves nonreligious do not care to be involved with either personal or corporate religion, but they do not mind if others find something of value in religion.

One teenager who said he was not religious still had a positive view of religion because it helped his aunt.

"She was heavily into drugs, then found God and has calmed down," he said. "So it gives a lot of people hope. I don't believe in pushing anything on people, but if they choose it, then great. It's all up to them" (126).

Smith says that religion "is generally viewed by most teenagers—religious and nonreligious alike—as something that simply is, that is just not the kind of thing worth getting worked up about" (124). He concludes that the vast majority of U.S. teens view religion in a benignly positive light (124).

Southern Baptist teenagers hold very similar views about religion. As noted, however, their warm, positive feelings about their church do not always influence how they live or what they believe. The majority of Southern Baptist teenagers, 57 percent, believe many religions may be true, and more than a third of SBC students think it is OK to practice other religions. (See Table 8.) That probably explains why few talk about religion with their friends.

TABLE 8. OK TO PRACTICE YOUR RELIGION PLUS ANOTHER?

	Percent
OK to Practice Other Religions	36
Should Only Practice One Faith	49
Don't Know	3
Refused	1
Not Asked	11
Total	100

Source: National Study of Youth and Religion, 2002-3.

Youth ministry needs to capitalize on the benignly positive attitude teenagers have toward the church and help youth see how critical a personal relationship with Christ is to their lives.

The "Me" Focus of Teenagers' Faith

For most teenagers in America, religion is important, but it is not really a way of life. Many teenagers seem to believe that God is like a "genie in the lamp." He is always there when one needs Him, but He stays in the lamp until someone rubs it. Smith says that teenagers see God as a counselor, someone who is always ready to assist in times of trouble. He is not the kind of deity, however, who demands commitment or obedience. One teenager was asked, "What good has God done in your life?" The teen responded, "I have a house, parents, I have the Internet, I have a phone, I have cable" (135). Teenagers seem to see religion as a means for them to get what they want to keep them happy. They pray, not to commune with God, but because it makes them feel good.

A 14-year-old boy told an interviewer, "Faith is very important, I pray to God to help me with sports and school and stuff and He hasn't let me down yet, so I think it helps you" (148). With this view of religion and God, what will this boy, and others like him, believe about their faith when life's problems arise?

Among Southern Baptist teenagers, 72 percent said their faith was either extremely important or very important in shaping their daily lives. An additional 20 percent said faith is somewhat important to the way they live. At first glance those numbers are encouraging. When asked how they decide what is right or wrong in difficult situations, however, only 31 percent said they turned to God or the Scriptures. Almost an identical percentage said they decided what was right or wrong based on whether it made them feel happy or helped them to get ahead in life. (See Table 9.) That means about a third of our teens see religion as a means to a particular end—being happy.

Southern Baptists want to see lives transformed, but that does not seem to be the goal of many youth. Our young people appear to be looking for ways their faith can benefit them personally and help them get ahead. On the other hand, they do not seem interested in any demands it might place on their lives.

TABLE 9. HOW TO DECIDE RIGHT/WRONG IN SITUATIONS?

	Percent
Makes me feel happy	22
Helps me get ahead	10
Follows advice of adult	36
God or Scripture says is right	31
Don't Know	1
Total	100

Source: National Study of Youth and Religion, 2002-3.

It is critical that we help teenagers understand what Jesus meant when He said, "I have told you these things, so that in me you may have peace. In this world you will have trouble. But take heart! I have overcome the world" (John 16:33, NIV). True happiness and fulfillment can be found only in obeying the commands of Jesus and living according to His plan.

Teenagers and Culture

American culture appears to have a definite influence on the religious views and practices of teenagers. Public schools teach teens to be tolerant and nonoffensive when it comes to anything religious and to be accepting of all cultural differences. The NSYR reported that most teenagers said their "teachers avoid discussing religion like the plague" (161) This factor alone, the researchers reported, made it difficult for adolescents even to admit that they held religious views that might be considered intolerant—for example, that they believe their religion is the one true religion, and particularly that they think some people will go to hell.

American culture teaches teenagers that an individual should not judge anyone or anything in general because each person has the right to decide for himself or herself what is true. This approach leads to the view that we should not only accept what others believe as being good for them, but we also should affirm them in their beliefs. Adolescents adsorb these views of society and fear being very dogmatic about what they believe (175).

The media is another area of American culture that challenges teens to move away from the things they have been taught in their religious training. One message of the media is that sex is so thrilling and hormones so raging that teens should practice what they consider "safe" sex. Rather than discussing the possibility (or even the benefits) of sexual abstinence, the popular assumption is that "everybody's doing it." This assumption that teens are going to have sex before marriage provides additional momentum to movements promoting "safe sex" as the most logical way teenagers can protect themselves.

The National Study of Youth and Religion revealed that in this capitalistic society, authority increasingly resides not in the church or the Scriptures, but in the individual. Religion is just one of many products that can satisfy the subjective needs, tastes, and wants of an individual. Religion thus becomes increasingly individualistic (177). Many of the adolescents interviewed in the survey declared that religion was "extremely important" in their lives; but at the same time, they considered taking part in church functions a nice thing to do when feasible or convenient. Homework, events, friends, television, and other diversions received higher preference than church attendance.

As noted, the drive toward tolerance in our society has had an amazing impact on teenagers' perceptions of truth and doctrine. For example, just 36.4 percent of Southern Baptist teenagers believe that Christianity is the only true religion. (See Table 10.)

TABLE 10. WHICH COMES CLOSEST TO YOUR OWN VIEWS?

	Percent
Only One Religion Is True	36
Many Religions May Be True	57
There Is Very Little Truth in Any Religion	5
Don't Know	2
Refused	Less than 1
Total	100.0

Source: National Study of Youth and Religion, 2002-3.

The cultural watering down of Christ as the exclusive door to salvation also has had a trickle down effect on the day-to-day morals of American teenagers. The following statistics related to Southern Baptist teenagers reveal the degree of culture's influence on how youth view life and morality outside the church walls.

- 58 percent admitted to cheating at least some in school.
- 57 percent said it is OK for couples without children to divorce.
- 34 percent said it is not necessary to wait until marriage for sex.
- 36 percent did not believe there are fixed moral standards.
- 33 percent believed you should not try to convert others.
- 41 percent would live with a romantic partner before marriage.
- 34 percent admitted to drinking alcohol.
- 22 percent admitted to having engaged in oral sex.
- 25 percent admitted to having experienced sexual intercourse.

Many things discussed in this chapter are reasons for concern. Some findings, however, should give parents and adult leaders a greater sense of hope. The majority of Southern Baptist teenagers enjoy the church, find it warm and accepting, and feel it informs them. They also value what they are taught by their parents and caring adults in the church. These are positive signs, but it is up to leaders and families to capitalize on these truths. Southern Baptist teenagers value the opinions of the adults they respect, so these adults need to help youth mature in Christ by exemplifying personal faith in action.

"This book of the law shall not depart from your mouth, but you shall meditate on it day and night, so that you may be careful to do according to all that is written in it; for then you will make your way prosperous, and then you will have success" (Josh. 1:8-9, NASB).

THE IMPLICATIONS

Karen Jones

In an effort to keep teenagers involved in the life of the church, some leaders have increasingly watered down practices and principles so as not to alienate or bore them. They want teenagers to enjoy their experience in the youth ministry. They want them to invite their friends and to remain active members of the group. To accomplish this, some have relied on trendy methods and imitated cultural models which may or may not contribute to spiritual formation and Christlike growth.

Some leaders have often shied away from the hard work of "training in righteousness" in favor of an easier agenda of "playing with popularity." They have tacitly accepted the notion that simply being with other like-minded teens in a Christian-friendly environment will somehow transform them into mature Christians, able to live out their faith.

Our task as parents and youth leaders is too critical to leave the outcome up to chance. As men and women called by God to the holy task of youth ministry, we must strategically choose ministry models and practices that lead teenagers to a deeper commitment to the faith which should be evident in all aspects of their lives. This means we must engage in the difficult task of developing sound curriculum strategies, appropriating effective ministry models, and thoroughly evaluating our motives, practices, and outcomes in light of our spiritual mission.

Bible as Core Curriculum

Teenagers are capable of making and keeping strong commitments and of accepting and fulfilling astonishing tasks. They want to be challenged more than they want to be entertained. They want to believe that their lives have meaning and purpose; they want to realize significance and experience success. Our ministry practices must provide them with the opportunity to realize these desires.

We know that the key to meaning, purpose, and significance is found in living in relationship with Jesus Christ and becoming conformed to His image. Our teenagers are searching for this key—not stories about the key, not sell jobs on the importance of the key. They want actual, tangible possession of the key. Our challenge is to give them that possession to equip them to live as fully-devoted followers of Jesus Christ.

All too often in our ministries we are tempted to fall back on reiterating biblical truths and principles that speak directly to important issues, to cite Scripture, and expect teenagers to obey simply because "the Bible says so." Yes, the authority of Scripture is reason enough to implement its teachings; but if teenagers don't know what the Bible says and what it means or don't automatically accept its authority, how do we bring about transformation and change in their lives?

It is similar to trying to converse with someone who doesn't speak our language. In an effort to be understood, we simply speak louder. The message we are trying to communicate remains a mystery, even though our raised voices may have gained us a larger audience!

Christian Smith has concluded that "most U.S. teens have a difficult-to-impossible time explaining what they believe, what it means, and what the implications of their beliefs are for their lives" (262). How can we expect teenagers to articulate their faith or make sound theological decisions when they have never been taught to think theologically? How can they express what they believe when they have only been exposed to the SparkNotes version of the Bible?

We have all too often given them the equivalent of a movie preview and expected them to critique the main characters, analyze the plot, and make application of the central theme to all of life. As obvious as it may seem, (somewhat like offering a "Sunday School answer" to an important, complex, question), it is crucial that we realize the absolute importance of centering and grounding our ministries upon the absolute authority of the Bible. This means that we must engage teenagers in a comprehensive, ongoing study of the entirety of God's Word and actively challenge them to live out biblical truth.

Southern Baptists have been referred to as a "people of the Book" because of our historic emphasis on the value of the Bible. While we still affirm that position, our ministry practices don't always measure up to our ideals, especially in student ministry. There are key passages and books that we faithfully teach, but large portions of Scripture that we overlook or only mention in passing. Our teenagers rarely complete an in-depth study of the entire Bible, even if they participate in our ministries for a full six years. Whether it is intentional or not, the result is the same; our teenagers often leave our ministries with an incomplete understanding of biblical truth.

This might be one explanation for why our teenagers are less involved socially or politically than non-Southern Baptist teenagers. For example: we passionately teach the absolute truth of salvation by faith and not by works, but we are less enthusiastic when addressing the importance of works as proof of our faith. Our teenagers are taught to love their neighbor and help those in need, but they may view these actions as merely good options and not necessary evidence of their faith.

Ask yourself:
- How much time do we spend studying the Bible in our ministry?
- Do we use a curriculum resource that includes a comprehensive study of the Bible?
- Do we expect teens to bring Bibles with them to youth meetings?
- Do we actually read from the Bible during our meeting times?
- Do we encourage teenagers to read the Bible outside of our meeting times?
- Do we provide teenagers with a Bible reading/study guide that is developmentally appropriate and also challenging?
- Do we have a system in place to evaluate whether or not our teenagers are studying the Bible on their own?
- Do I enlist Bible study leaders/teachers that are effective in communicating biblical truth?
- Do I model the importance of Bible study?
- Do I defer to the Bible as the source of authority?

As teenagers learn to value reading and studying the Bible in a ministry setting, they will begin to develop the practice of reading the Bible on their own. If a commitment to reading the Bible is not a significant part of our ministries, how can we expect teenagers to make and keep a commitment to personal Bible study?

Self-Esteem

Self-esteem issues are pervasive in our society and have dominated the educational practices of this generation of teenagers. They have received trophies for participating in sports competitions, regardless of whether they were first or last. They have been promoted, whether they have mastered a subject or not. They have been in schools which have refused to give failing grades and have been parented by adults who were afraid to say no. Young competitors on national reality shows refuse to accept the decisions of the judges when their talent is criticized, and some teachers refuse to use red pens because of the perceived damage to the self-esteem of the teenagers.

Society has been so fearful of damaging self-esteem that our teenagers now have a hard time accepting objective standards of absolute truth. This is one major area of concern for student ministers.

In a world where everyone's opinion is valued equally, for fear of damaging someone's self-esteem or being considered intolerant, how can we teach teenagers the difference between right and wrong? How can we help them understand that salvation only comes through Christ, that God isn't a bigot, that His commands are more than suggestions, and that He is the ultimate Judge of right and wrong—not a committee of our peers?

While not a quick fix, the long-term solution is to teach teenagers that there are biblical standards of right and wrong that are constant, objective, and universal. Youth ministers must not shy away from teaching absolute truth, which will impact teenagers' attitudes and influence the decisions they make in their daily lives.

Holding High the Truth

The pervasive focus on self-esteem in our society has found a foothold in our ministry practices as well. We avoid labeling behaviors and attitudes as sinful because they might offend teenagers or cause them to feel poorly about themselves. We fear that confronting wrong beliefs or behaviors might discourage teenagers or cause them to feel defeated.

This concern over damaging the self-esteem of our teenagers can also keep us from affirming teenagers who have exhibited strong Christian commitments or who have made tough stands for Christ. We are afraid that less committed teenagers may feel left out, feel like failures, or see themselves as "bad Christians." We obviously want to nurture and love our teenagers and to do all we can to model forgiveness and grace; but this should not cause us to ignore sin or accept personal opinions that contradict biblical teachings.

Research does exist to show a positive correlation between religious commitment and self-esteem.[6] At the same time, our main concern is not to help teenagers feel good about themselves. Our responsibility is to lead them into a saving relationship with Christ and to nurture them as they are transformed into His image.

Developing as a disciple involves growing in Christlikeness, which, in turn, includes a recognition and rejection of sin. As student ministers, we must engage in practices that affirm the worth of all persons as unique creations of a personal God, while at the same time calling them to personal holiness. Spiritual growth cannot happen in the lives of our teenagers if we avoid confronting sin for fear of damaging self-esteem.

Affirmation

It is extremely important, however, for student ministers to realize that teens are vulnerable as they are developing their sense of identity. They are in desperate need of validation and acceptance. We must incarnate God's love for all persons—a love that is most evident in Christ's sacrifice for our sin. This means accepting and loving all teenagers, even those who are hard to love. Purposeful praise and appropriate affirmation are also powerful means of encouraging spiritual growth and reinforcing right behavior.

Blanket, indiscriminate praise can prove detrimental, however. It can send mixed messages to teenagers who are learning what it means to live as a follower of Christ. Our praise must ring true and be focused on the qualities of personhood and not on extraneous characteristics. Affirming Christlike behaviors in our teenagers also provides a tangible standard for which others can strive. It gives them a concrete picture of what it means to live out a specific Christian principle.

We must also be cautious in this type of affirmation so that we don't somehow cultivate a climate in which teenagers feel that they are accepted when they live out their faith, but will be rejected when they let us down. Recognizing and admitting our own failures can be a powerful model to our teenagers of how to deal with personal shortcomings while striving for conformity to the image of Christ.

Confrontation

It is generally easier for student ministers to affirm than to confront. A love for teenagers is an important qualification and indicator of a call to ministry, which makes affirmation and praise a natural action.

However, love also requires discipline and confrontation as shown in the actions and words of Christ. He showed compassion and love to the woman caught in adultery when He rescued her from her accusers, but He also went a step further. He admonished her to turn away from her sinful actions (John 8:1-11).

When the rich young ruler asked Jesus what he should do to gain eternal life, Jesus responded with a task that the young man could not accept. Jesus did not lower His standards for the man, even though it meant watching him walk away. Instead, He stood firmly by the truth. He did not allow His love for the man or His desire to build the kingdom to cause Him to waver on His principles (Matt. 19:16-22).

In the final days of His earthly ministry, when Jesus told His disciples to keep watch while He prayed in the garden of Gethsemane, they fell asleep. Jesus was disappointed when He found them, and confronted Peter directly, *"Could you men not keep watch with me for one hour?"* (Matt. 26:36-41, NIV). Again, even near the end of His time on earth, Jesus continued to teach in a way that combined true love with a spirit of discipline and, when necessary, confrontation.

There is no question that Jesus is our model for how to love and affirm, but we must also look to His life for examples of how and when to confront. Teenagers learn best in a climate of freedom where they know they are valued and their beliefs, opinions, and questions will not be ridiculed or rejected outrightly. Acceptance of the individual does not mean, however, that all opinions and beliefs are accepted without critical and biblical examination.

Honest Discussion

If we do not provide a climate in which our teenagers can honestly express themselves, we may not be aware of errors in their thinking or have the chance to correct wrong doctrine. According to Smith, our teenagers will face challenging and unorthodox beliefs once they leave our ministries and enter college or the workplace. If they have not had the chance to examine and discuss such ideas from a Christian world-view, in the light of biblical truth, they will be more likely to become confused about what they believe. As a result, they will find themselves more vulnerable to the prevailing mind-set of the culture.

When we remain silent in the face of wrong beliefs or actions, willful disobedience, or hurtful attitudes or speech, our silence may be interpreted as acceptance. Student ministers must call teenagers to the truth in action, attitude, belief, and speech.

It requires patience and practice to accept and affirm the worth of all teenagers, while also balancing discipline and engaging in graceful confrontation. Faithfulness to our mission, however, demands that we make the investment. God has given us the responsibility, along with parents, of guiding and nurturing the faith development of our teenagers, and we are in a unique position of influence in their lives.

Smith's research reminds us that "adults inescapably exercise immense influence in the lives of teens—positive and negative, passive and active. The question therefore is not whether adults exert influence, but rather what kinds of influence they exert."[7]

Discovery of Giftedness

An outstanding Southern Baptist educator, Findley B. Edge, has written that a student "learns in and from the group whose approval he seeks" and that "those who learn best are those who have a vision of what life is all about and who have worthy goals."[8] One of the most effective ways to nurture a sense of purpose and worth in our teenagers is to help them understand their giftedness and their uniqueness in Christ. When teenagers realize that they really can contribute to God's kingdom and make a significant difference, they are more likely to live out their God-given potential.

The search for purpose and significance in life is a universal human quest, even more pronounced in adolescence. When teenagers begin to uncover the gifts and talents God has given them and recognize tangible ways they can use those abilities and gifts, they begin to believe and more fully understand what it means to be part of the body of Christ. The meaning of passages such as Romans 12, 1 Corinthians 12, and Ephesians 4—which speak about the integral relationship of all parts of the body—come alive to teenagers when they begin to see themselves as valuable, gifted, members of the church.

All persons desire and need to feel valued. It is discouraging to work at a task in which we feel inadequate or unnecessary. It is even more demotivating to be ignored. Teenagers who are passive members of a youth group have little motivation to remain active if they believe their presence doesn't matter.

According to Smith and the NSYR research team, "religious faith and practice in American teenagers' lives operate in a social and institutional environment that is highly competitive for time, attention, and energy. Religious interests and values in teens' lives typically compete against those of school, homework, television, other media, sports, romantic relationships, paid work, and so forth. Indeed, in many adolescents' lives, religion occupies a quite weak and often losing position among these competing influences."[9]

This is especially true as teens get older. They often make choices about how to invest their time based on the perceived relevance of the activity in relation to their personal goals or the sense of community they will experience.

When teenagers are given significant ministry and leadership opportunities that are aligned with their areas of strength, their chances of gaining acceptance and approval are maximized. They begin to see their active participation as meaningful and rewarding. Regardless of whether or not they receive outside praise or affirmation, they begin to experience the inner satisfaction that comes with successfully completing a task or accomplishing a mission.

As student ministers, we must enable our teenagers to find this sense of purpose by helping them discover their identity in Christ. We also need to make sure we are empowering them to serve in accordance with their unique abilities and gifts. Utilizing lead teams in ministry planning and implementation is one way to involve teenagers in leadership and active service.

Ask yourself:

- Are all teenagers accepted in our ministry?
- Do all teenagers know they are loved and valued in our ministry?
- Do I intentionally affirm and encourage our teenagers?
- Do I model acceptance and Christlike love?
- Do I recognize and affirm teenagers' growth in faith?
- Do we lovingly confront teenagers' actions, attitudes, or speech when necessary?
- Do we uphold standards we have set in our ministry?
- Do we teach principles of absolute truth which are constant, objective, and universal?
- Do we help our teenagers discover their spiritual gifts?
- Do we engage our teenagers in ministry leadership tasks that allow them to use their gifts in service?

Student ministers must nurture a sense of worth in all teenagers that is grounded in the unconditional love of Christ. As teenagers begin to mature in their faith, they will also grow in their self-understanding and self-acceptance. Self-confidence comes from an understanding of their worth in Christ. It empowers teenagers to reach out in love to others, contributing to a growing, vibrant student ministry that is more community than clique.

Transformational Teaching

The role of the student minister is described in many different ways: coach, counselor, friend, minister, pastor, shepherd, and spiritual guide. The title that captures the spirit of each of these labels and most accurately describes the central task of the student minister, however, is that of teacher. Jesus Himself was referred to as *Teacher* more than by any other title.

Teachers have the task of facilitating learning, and learning means changing: acquiring new information, understanding concepts and principles, mastering new skills, adopting new attitudes or values. All of these changes are ways of learning. Whether student ministers view themselves primarily as coaches or counselors, their primary goal is to work with God in bringing about spiritual transformation in the lives of their teenagers.

With this understanding of teaching and learning, the label "transformational teaching" may sound redundant. Unfortunately, much of what passes for teaching in student ministry falls short of bringing about transformation in the lives of teenagers.

This is evident in the following research conclusion from Christian Smith, "most religious teenagers' opinions and views—one can hardly call them worldviews—are vague, limited, and often quite at variance with the actual teachings of their own religions. In the end, many teenagers know abundant details about the lives of favorite musicians and televisions stars or about what it takes to get into a good college, but most turn out to be not very clear on who Moses and Jesus were. This suggests that a strong, visible, salient, or intentional faith is not operating in the foreground of most teenagers' lives" (134).

Our teaching is often shallow and ineffective because we fail to take into account the ability of our teenagers to learn and their desire to be challenged and engaged. If we can commit ourselves to effective strategies of transformational teaching and take seriously our role as change agents, we will begin to develop teenagers conformed to the image of Christ who can articulate their faith and can have a powerful impact on their culture.

Methodology

Teenagers need to be involved in active learning that engages them cognitively and also allows them to move and interact socially. We tend to avoid lectures in our teaching because we think they will bore our teenagers. It is true that one-way communication can often be ineffective, especially if we lack preparation or speak over the heads of our audience. As a result of our hesitancy to bore teenagers and our desire to involve them in the learning process, we may have relied too heavily in the past on group discussion and poorly planned small group activities that failed to challenge our teenagers or lead them to discover significant biblical truths.

We must recognize that people learn best in different ways, and we need to incorporate a variety of methodologies in our teaching, including lecture. This method of teaching is actually the most flexible and can be combined with a variety of other techniques to take learning to deeper levels.

Consider the following situations for which lecture is a viable means of teaching: when there is a lot of important information or specific facts that need to be communicated; when a specific problem or issue needs to be addressed clearly; when you want to motivate or inspire your teenagers toward a specific goal or challenge; when there are many different points of view about a topic or issue that need to be presented; when you want to set the stage for a topic; or when you want to review the important points of a learning session. If a session is getting out of control or taking a turn down a wrong path, lecture can be used to get a session back on track.

Using the lecture method does not mean that the teacher talks and the teenagers listen. A skilled teacher incorporates intriguing illustrations, uses conversation in the presentation, mixes in methods of involvement, and asks probing questions in the midst of the lecture. All too often we expect teenagers to interact around a topic about which they have little information or experience.

By presenting them with a core component through our use of lecture, we can take them much deeper in their discussion and in their learning. The effective use of lecture requires us to have a clear focus in our message with a clear destination in mind before we begin. It is important to outline a specific goal and key points, and then to add effective illustrations as you plan.

There are definite limitations to the use of lecture that must be considered. It is a method that works better with a large group than a small one, but when the group is too large it is very difficult to keep everyone engaged. Using a master teacher approach, in which a large group lecture is followed by small breakout groups, can provide teenagers with opportunities to dig deeper into the lesson's content on a more personal level and critically analyze the concepts presented. Smaller groupings of teenagers are advantageous in that everyone can have the opportunity to interact and participate in the learning process.

Jesus taught large crowds, but most of His teaching was directed at a small group of twelve. One-to-one teaching and mentoring are powerful and provide maximum opportunities for adults to directly impact the lives of teenagers, but the dynamics of the small group allow teenagers to learn from, challenge, and sharpen one another as well.

Using questions in our teaching, whether incorporated into a lecture or assigned to small groups for discussion, is a definite skill that requires careful planning. Yes-or-no questions or questions that can be answered with little thought are not very helpful in developing critical thinking in our teenagers. We want them to wrestle with their beliefs, to analyze competing views and values, and to construct their own faith story based on solid biblical truth. Teenagers cannot be expected to articulate their faith in the midst of a hostile culture if they have never had to do the hard work of theological reflection in a nurturing environment. The body of Christ should be willing to provide that environment.

Probing questions, mock debates, realistic case studies, and honest discussion about significant or controversial issues can prepare teenagers for life. They should always be asked to ground their opinions and decisions in biblical truth. Why do they respond they way they do? Can they defend their actions or positions?

The "What Would Jesus Do?" marketing extravaganza probably anesthetized many teenagers to the very real significance of that crucial question. For all decisions and in all situations, they should be led to discover from a biblical perspective how the Savior would respond to those circumstances. Using this type of test in a creative way can draw teenagers into critical reflection and analysis.

Learning is more likely to occur when teenagers are given the opportunity to discover and experience truth than when they are taught in a passive style. Jesus used the project approach with His learners. He sent them out into the surrounding culture with a specific learning task, then He brought them back together for a time of debriefing. As a result, He helped them make sense of what they observed and experienced. (Luke 10:1-24 is one example of this teaching method.)

Student ministers can appropriate this same method through mission trips, service projects, or focused retreats that have specifically identified educational and spiritual growth goals.

Learning through Service

Our teenagers benefit in many ways from being involved in volunteer ministries or mission projects. These benefits include a deeper religious faith, an increase in leadership abilities and self-confidence, an elevated commitment to church and missions, an increased understanding of the church's role in society, a growing sense of community with other believers, the development of cultural sensitivity and appreciation, greater self-esteem and self-concept, and a growing dependence on God.

Teaching teenagers through service projects can also increase youth group cohesion and a commitment to service. Other group benefits include the application of learning to real life, the empowerment of teenagers for leadership, and the shift in role expectations of adult leaders from presenters of information to facilitators. Churches that provide opportunities for teenagers to become involved in ministry are also giving them a chance to explore and use their gifts and talents.

Student ministers must provide opportunities for teenagers to maximize their learning by providing opportunities to critically reflect on their experiences through small group discussions, journaling, and corporate worship. Involvement itself does not guarantee that teenagers will learn or be changed, however, since learning is not automatic.

Not only does reflection help solidify the learning that takes place, but it can actually multiply the commitment of teenagers to missions and ministry. This type of reflection should raise questions that cause teenagers to interpret their experiences in the light of biblical truth. Their experiences and interaction with the world can lead to deeper self-examination related to social justice and their responsibility as Christians in serving humanity as ambassadors for Christ.

This approach to teaching and learning is also beneficial in helping teenagers discover and deepen their personal faith through action. In the end, teenagers may grasp a better of understanding of how the biblical views they verbally affirm about faith and belief should be guiding their behavior and attitudes.

Implications for Parent Ministry

Smith's study reminds us that "the single most important social influence on the religious and spiritual lives of adolescents is their parents" (261). If student ministers sincerely desire to impact the lives of their teenagers, they must invest in a comprehensive ministry with parents. This means involving parents in decision making through lead teams and focus groups, enlisting them to serve as ministry volunteers, soliciting their prayer support, and inviting them to participate in various ministry projects and student events.

Parents also need very practical help in knowing how to live out their faith commitments and nurture their own spiritual growth. As Smith states, parents "will get what they are," so we must intentionally help parents become godly persons and positive role models (261). This may take the form of spiritual retreats, parent-to-parent mentoring, or accountability groups. The senior pastor, leaders in adult ministries, and the youth minister should come together to craft experiences that deepen the walk parents experience with Christ.

Student ministers can provide parents with resources and opportunities to help them connect with their teens, listen to them, nurture them, and talk with them about faith issues. Leaders can offer verbal and prayer support for parents in the presence of teenagers and encourage strong family bonds that contribute to enriched relationships between parents and teens. Parents can reinforce the teaching that takes place within the student ministry when they are aware of its goals and current emphases.

Information presented throughout this book has focused on the importance of training parents for parenting and for spiritual leadership. Other ministries that can bless families include:

- Intensive Parenting Courses. These can be small-group studies lasting several weeks.
- Parent and Youth Dialogs. These allow the generations to hear from and learn from each other.
- Parent and Youth Retreats. These can include a plan where strong families "adopt" youth whose parents will not participate.
- Parent Appreciation Banquets. These involve teenagers decorating, cooking, serving, and entertaining as a way to say thanks to their parents.
- Parent and Youth Fellowship. In reality, almost any youth recreation event can be adapted and made into a family event.
- Parent and Youth Mission Projects. These can be something as simple as an outreach to the community or as complex as a mission trip to another part of the world.

Conclusion

Student ministries and parents must begin to work hand in hand in nurturing the spiritual lives of teenagers. In other words, both must confront error, affirm and love unconditionally, stand on the truth of God without compromise, and engage teenagers in thoughtful discussion and critical reflection that will lead to a deeper understanding and commitment to Christ.

ENDNOTES

1. Steve Rabey, *In Search of Authentic Faith: How Emerging Generations Are Transforming the Church* (Waterbrook Press, Colorado Springs, 2001), 11.

2. Christian Smith with Melinda Lundquist Denton, *Soul Searching: The Religious and Spiritual Lives of American Teenagers* (Oxford University Press, New York, 2005), 161.

3. George Barna, *Generation Next* (Regal Books, Ventura, CA, 1995), 80.

4. Christian Smith, Robert Faris, and Melinda Lundquist Denton, "Are American Youth Alienated from Organized Religion," in *A Research Report of the National Study of Youth and Religion*, Number 6 (2004), 19-20.

5. Smith and Denton, 39.

6. Howard M. Bahr and Thomas K. Martin, " 'And Thy Neighbor as Thyself': Self-Esteem and Faith in People as Correlates of Religiosity and Family Solidarity Among Middletown High School Students," *Journal for the Scientific Study of Religion* 22 (1983), 132.

7 Smith and Denton, 28.

8. Findley B. Edge, *Teaching for Results,* revised edition (Broadman & Holman Publishers, Nashville, TN, 1995), 37-8.

9. Smith and Denton, 28.

Releasing Teenagers to the Kingdom

GOD WANTS TEENAGERS WHO EMBODY HIS NAME, thus reflecting His character. He wants teenagers who obey His Word. He wants teenagers to take His message to the nations—calling upon all people groups to align themselves with God's rule and reign. He promises to bless kingdom teenagers in order that all the nations of the earth might be drawn to Him.

Releasing Kingdom Teenagers for Short-Term Missions

God calls some Christians to make missions their life vocation. God calls every Christian to join Him in evangelizing the world. The Great Commission is a commission to every Christian, young and old.

God calls every child, teenager, and adult to short-term missions. That fact is not debatable. The only question is, will those He calls be obedient? As youth leaders and parents, we need to encourage obedience in the area of missions. We need to emphasize both the responsibility to go and the spiritual value of going, such as the following:

VALUES OF SHORT-TERM MISSIONS INVOLVEMENT

1. Obedience to sovereign God.
2. Freedom from the nagging guilt that accompanies disobedience.
3. Motivation for growth in the Christian disciplines.
4. Deeper sensitivity to institutionalized injustice.
5. Appreciation for one's blessings.
6. Deeper bond with mature Christian leaders and peers.
7. More humility.
8. More positive attitude toward sacrifice and generosity.
9. Greater affection for people of other cultures and races.
10. Deeper faith from watching God do what only He can do.
11. Deeper faith in the power of prayer.
12. Joy from seeing lives transformed, churches established, and the kingdom expanded.

This Generation in This Generation by This Generation

In some ways, the youth of the world have become a people group. Through the influence of movies and television, youth across the globe are beginning to dress alike and talk alike. They are beginning to see the world in similar ways.

Most of the two billion teenagers of the world are unreached. Traditional missionary strategies have been more effective in reaching children and adults than teenagers, and the clock is ticking. Of those youth who reach age 18 without accepting Christ as Savior, nine out of 10 will spend eternity in hell.

Before they begin an eternity separated from God, though, these billions of lost students will harm the world in many ways. They will become leaders in government, business, education, science, the military, and many other arenas of life. With no personal faith and no core values, their influence will drag culture down even further than it is today. In contrast, if those individuals are reached with the gospel, their positions in the future can become ministries that can change the world.

The only viable strategy for reaching large numbers of lost youth worldwide is to mobilize Christian middle schoolers, high schoolers, and collegians to win their peers. For example, American young people have several advantages as evangelists:

1. Many international students are fascinated with western culture and entertainment. As a result, they are drawn to American students who live in that culture.
2. Many international students believe knowing English is an advantage in life. They value any opportunities they get to practice their English skills with American students.
3. Many international students plan to travel to the United States some day and consider it an advantage to find out more about the country from American students.
4. American Christian teenagers do not seem as daunting to students in other countries as "religious" adults.
5. American Christian teenagers may find it easier to establish relationships with someone who shares their age and interests.

In addition to these advantages, there are several spiritual realities with which we must come to grips in this issue. Again, these point back to both our responsibility to reach others and our willingness to obey the clear teaching of Christ.

- *We must win this generation.* They matter to God. They are central to His purposes, and they will shape the world for good or ill.
- *We must win this generation in this generation.* We cannot allow millions to slip into eternity without Christ. We must win them now, before they reach adulthood.
- *We must win this generation in this generation by this generation.* All Christians—young or old—can and should lead a teenager to Christ. But the most efficient strategy for winning them quickly and in large numbers must center on mobilizing our own adolescents to reach their peers around the world.

Calling Out Every Student to Go on an Extended Mission While Young

The time has come for leaders and parents to challenge their teenagers to invest at least a summer, semester, or year in full-time mission work while they are young.

Currently, typical high school students participate in two kinds of mission endeavors. In some cases, they help with local mission projects lasting a day. More commonly, they take part in summer mission trips lasting about a week. These are valuable experiences that always will have a place in ministry.

At the same time, leaders and parents recognize that the degree and depth of life transformation during such brief experiences must be somewhat limited. That is why students should be challenged to take on longer tasks while they have the freedom and opportunity. The results can be even more transformational—for the student and for the culture he or she reaches for Christ.

All Go

An increasing number of Christian leaders now are challenging all students to invest a summer, semester, or year in front-line missions service. This usually will mean going to a mission point alone or with a friend rather than with a church group. In many cases, students will serve alongside career missionaries in North America or around the world. Leaders dream of a day when it will be normative for most students to make this kind of commitment.

Leaders have come to see the potential that high school students have on the mission field. Many older high school students have the maturity and the spiritual strength to serve most of the summer. High school students in such settings have proved in recent years that they can be effective in missions roles—pulling their own weight and making a kingdom impact on lost communities.

This generation of students understands little about denominations, missions agencies, funding plans, or administrative processes. All they know is that they have a call from God to accomplish something bold and kingdom shaking. They will tend to follow any voice that promises to open those doors for them. Parents and church leaders will be most comfortable when those open doors for assignments include thorough support and supervision on the field, partnership with established career missionaries, and biblically sound doctrine.

Over the next few years, youth ministries that primarily stay in an entertainment mode with students will lose many of their strong teenagers to churches that provide a challenge. Students with a heart for God will move toward challenge wherever they can find it. For many, the greatest challenge they have been given so far is mowing the grass at home or setting the table for dinner. If one church only challenges students to help build the "world's longest banana split" and another church challenges students to invest a summer with an unreached people group, guess where the students will gravitate.

Future Changes

Leaders should look forward to the time when most grade schoolers will grow up already knowing they will be young missionaries some day. Such teenagers will become high school or college students who consistently seek to hear from God and enthusiastically await their time to go. Their public affirmation that the time has arrived may become one of the most common decisions at youth rallies and conferences.

Leaders can enjoy dreaming about the impact this new challenge will have on the church. Imagine 15 years from now in any church when most of the deacons and Bible teachers will have clear memories of the time they spent out on the front lines of missions. The spiritual climate of those churches will be completely different. In addition, returning students likely will show a lifetime willingness to join short-term mission projects (whether nearby or far away) and to support missions offerings.

If virtually every active member of church youth groups begins serving in missions while young, we should see a dramatic increase in the number of students hearing and responding to God's call to lifetime Christian vocations. For example, 18 out of 26 high school young men from Texas who did mission work in Kenya heard a call to lifetime Christian ministries.

The call to be a career missionary is reserved for a few. But in this era of the church, perhaps God intends to call out most Christian students to join Him full-time for a season to accelerate the harvest.

Saving Money to Fund This Adventure

Finances represent a potential challenge to this missions endeavor. If the majority of older high school and college students step forward to serve from a summer to a year, millions of dollars will be needed to cover their basic living expenses. Such funds do not exist in any denomination or organization.

Instead, leaders are challenging parents to begin savings accounts that some day will fund their teenagers' time of missions service. Ideally, accounts should be opened at the birth of a child. Even couples of modest means should be able to set up an automatic draft that would move $5 or more a month into that savings account.

Wise pastors can use baby dedications to point young couples in this direction. By handing the couple a small check from the church, he can invite them to open a savings account the next day for their baby's future missions adventure.

In the future, church members attending baby showers might choose to provide financial gifts for missions savings accounts. Similarly, members and relatives might make gifts to the accounts for birthdays, graduations, and other special times. Godly grandparents might sense God's leadership to make significant gifts to each of their grandchildren's accounts along the way.

Such a plan will result in tens of thousands of students reaching upper high school or college each year with all the funds they need to invest a summer or even a year in an inner-city neighborhood or international outpost.

At present, funding is a ceiling that prevents many from doing what they sense a call to do. If families save for their teenagers, there will be no ceilings at all.

Wise parents will allow even younger teenagers to earn money that can be placed into the child's missions savings account. When teenagers move into the adolescent years, they can be challenged to work as hard to save for their mission project as they would for a car. Obviously, where a teenager's money is his heart will be also.

Family savings accounts can mean that in 16 years we will see students ready to serve who have all the resources they need. But what about teenagers and collegians called by God to go now? If God wills for them to go now, He also will provide the resources they need.

Many parents are willing to make significant financial sacrifices to provide opportunities for their teenagers. When the local band is invited to march in the Thanksgiving Day Parade on national TV, when the school French club decides to go to Paris, when a student has had a lifetime dream to go to Space Camp, parents often make the sacrifices to open those doors. Godly parents will help many students gather funds for a trip this year.

Church members may be willing to help fund a mission trip—especially if they feel comfortable with the sending organization and the way the trip will be conducted. Grandparents and other relatives also are helping to fund students who feel called to go now.

Bottom line—families moving in the center of God's plans will find the resources they need.

Releasing Kingdom Teenagers to Face Risk and Even Martyrdom if Ordained by God

Any discussion of releasing teenagers to missions raises concerns for their safety. Here is an interesting question for church parents to consider.

TRUE OR FALSE

___ My teenager will be safer and better off if I dictate that he or she disobey God's will and plan to stay close to home.

Many Christian parents have clear memories of prayers they prayed at the birth of a child. Most told God they were dedicating that child to

His purposes. If fact, most affirmed that the child belonged to God and expressed gratitude for the opportunity to raise God's child.

Parents will have to pray those same prayers again when their teenager says she feels called to serve in a high-need neighborhood or a third-world country. In such a moment, the protective instincts of parenting inevitably collide with faith in the Father.

Parents have a responsibility to make sure their children serve with an agency or organization that has taken every prudent measure to ensure the safety of student missionaries. Parents have a responsibility to teach their teenagers how to minimize risks away from home. But in the end, godly parents must place the lives of their teenagers in the hands of the Father—just as they did in the delivery room.

Sacrifice is not a very American idea. An international missionary whose name cannot be revealed for security reasons has noted, "The American culture is one of entitlement that views safety, health, and security as fundamental rights, but that is not how Christians should think...We live in a culture that has trouble grasping delayed gratification, much less denied gratification. This is cultural orthodoxy and it is powerful. It is also delusional."[1]

Mark Matlock has it right:

"The purpose of God, not our comfort, is our goal. The will of God, not our pleasure, is our passion. That's the perspective that young people must have if they are going to be gripped with the heart of God for His cause, His message, and His calling. And that's the perspective that the parents of these young people must have if we are to impart that passion and equip them to serve God whole-heartedly."[2]

I attend Wedgwood Baptist Church in Fort Worth, Texas. For families with teenagers there, risk and martyrdom are not academic issues. On September 15, 1999, a gunman barged into a Wednesday night rally related to "See You at the Pole." Within minutes, he had gunned down seven students and leaders and had killed himself.

That horrific moment continues to be a daily part of the life of this church. As we gather to worship, we know that under the new carpet the blood of these faithful young soldiers remains. Sunday after Sunday we hold on to the truth that God establishes the church on the blood of the martyrs.

Wedgwood parents who lost teenagers sometimes read about parents who say, "My first responsibility is to protect my teenagers. I must prevent them from going on this mission project in order to keep them safe." The Wedgwood parents would gently ask, "What appears safer than having your kids in your own church auditorium on a Wednesday night?"

In reality, church auditoriums aren't safe anymore. Neither are cars or bedrooms. For the kingdom family, all that matters is making sure each family member is exactly where God has called him or her to be. From a heavenly perspective, the only safe place is in the center of God's will.

Churches that exist for the glory of God must release their teenagers to risk—and even the possibility of martyrdom—if sovereign God should so ordain.

Releasing Kingdom Teenagers for God's Purposes in Vocation

In the New International Version of the Bible, the familiar passage in Proverbs 22:6 reads: *"Train a child in the way he should go, and when he is old he will not turn from it."*

The Hebrew construction of this verse suggests that parents should train their children in accordance with the children's unique personality and unique life plan. The Darby Translation of the Bible says it this way: "Train up the child according to the tenor of his way." A Bible commentary interprets "the way" as "literally, 'his way,' that selected for him in which he should go."

A leader who sometimes serves as a spiritual mentor to the Dallas Cowboys football team once told me, "I spend the majority of the time trying to help those young dads know how to love and affirm sons in their homes who have no interest in football. I am trying to show them how to celebrate the gifts in music or art or dance their sons are discovering. I'm telling you, it's tough for them."

If parents try to make teenagers into what they cannot be, misery for both parent and teenager can be the only result. Church leaders need to help parents join God in discovering and then championing the unique "bent" He has given each teenager.

Possible Revival and the Completed Task

Note that the title of this section begins with the word *possible*. That choice is intentional because *possible* acknowledges the sovereignty of God. No author should suggest he knows revival is coming. Only God can know that.

Without a doubt, the United States deserves the judgment of God. This country has even exceeded the fallenness of the pagan nations of the Old Testament period. Someone has said with tongue in cheek, "If God does not launch judgment on America, He will have to apologize to Sodom and Gomorrah."

Yes, the United States deserves the judgment of God; but it is possible that out of His grace and mercy He will send revival instead. Since revival is at least a possibility, it merits discussion. But even this discussion should not suggest that revival is guaranteed.

Revival and Spiritual Awakening

Revival is an extraordinary movement of the Holy Spirit producing extraordinary results. God begins, at His choosing and timing, to break the hearts of those seeking Him. There is a profound sense of sin, the need for repentance, and the holiness of God. Believers confess sins openly, getting right with God and with others. As a result, the church is revived. This spills over to lost people, and the movement cannot be controlled because it is under God's control.

Hallmarks of Periods of Revival

Even though God-breathed revivals have been occurring over a period of several thousand years, they have much in common. Some of the basic characteristics include:

- A solemn sense of the presence of God
- Brokenness over sin
- Radical obedience
- Hunger for prayer
- Crossing of denominational lines without a loss of distinctives
- Strong belief in Scripture.

Spiritual awakening refers to a time when God transforms not only the church but also whole cultures and continents. Revivals alter the lives of individuals; awakenings alter the worldview of whole people groups or cultures.

Kingdom Youth Have Launched Most of the Great Revivals in History

God does exactly what He chooses to do. He never is bound by the expectations of others or even by ways He has acted in the past. What He has done in the past is no guarantee of what He will do in the future. While it is true that He has launched most major revivals through youth and young adults, He might choose to launch the next one through preschoolers or senior adults. He is sovereign.

At the same time, watching how He has moved in the past might cast light on how the next great revival will begin. Parents must take note of the fact that youth and young adults have launched most of the great revivals of history. Parents may very well have the next revival generation living in their homes.

God's ways are beyond understanding, but it is interesting to guess why He turns to the young to launch revival. Perhaps God considers some of the following realities.

- Youth are at a point developmentally when they have more courage than fear.
- Youth are not locked into old ways of thinking.
- Youth have a built-in distrust for the status quo and are intrigued with change.
- Youth, not shouldering adult obligations, have more freedom with their time and resources.
- Youth have not lost the close tie between faith and emotions.
- Youth love community and feeling part of powerful movements.
- Youth have a strong sense of justice and have not yet sold their souls to the culture.

There are hundreds of stories of God raising up older teenagers and what we now call collegians to launch revival.

There Are Signs God Is Moving in This Generation of Students

Those who have survived a lightning strike often report a tingly feeling just before being hit. An increasing number of youth leaders are having similar feelings right now, and it has nothing to do with the weather. Many believe revival and a sweeping awakening could come in the near future. They also believe teenagers and collegians might be at the forefront of that movement.

Here are indications God is moving in this generation of students.

- The desire of an increasing number of students to serve on the front lines of missions while young.
- The intensity with which many Christian students are practicing worship.
- The continuing expansion of student prayer movements, symbolized by praying around their school flagpoles.
- Spreading commitment to moral purity, symbolized in the international growth of the *True Love Waits®* movement.
- The zeal of an increasing number of students to take their schools for Christ.

Adults Can Help Their Teenagers Raise Their Sails for Revival

Periods of revival and awakening are sovereign acts of God. They cannot be orchestrated by believers, and there is no formula for making God behave in a certain way or on a certain schedule.

Leaders can't make the winds of revival and awakening blow, but they can set the sails. If the winds do not blow in this day, nothing is lost. But if they raise the sails and the winds do blow, then glorious things will happen. Here is what leaders can do.

FIRST STEP

The most important step in preparing teenagers for revival is to set the sails in the leader's own life. Nothing can have greater impact on teenage believers than living with parents who are experiencing a fresh movement of God in their own lives. The second most powerful experience they can have is experiencing life with leaders whose sails are up.

SECOND STEP

The second most important step in preparing teenagers for revival is to pray for them and to lead others to pray for and with them. At times, God chooses to move in response to the concerted, fervent, extended prayers of His people. If the leaders and parents in a church are not gathering to pray fervently over their teenagers, their sails are down.

THIRD STEP

The third most important step in preparing teenagers is to tell them about the movement of God in the past (1 Chron. 16:19, Ps. 105:1.) From Scripture, from historical accounts, and from a host of current stories, leaders need to build into teenagers and collegians a confidence in God and in what He can do through their generation. Telling the stories of revival helps raise sails for what He may be about to do again.

What a glorious time to be a leader or a parent with teenagers. Adults may be sharing life with those among whom God is about to do something wonderful.

143

Kingdom Students May Carry the Gospel to the Last People Groups

Revival first falls on the church. Once the church is revived, the impact spreads. God ordains some revivals to spread across localities. He ordains other revivals to spread across countries and even continents.

Teenagers and young adults swept up in revival quickly turn their attention to the lost. Most begin to evangelize friends and family close by. Some carry the gospel far away. Some make missions their life work. Others earn their living by secular means, but they continue to be on mission all of their lives. At times God has ordained that revivals should launch major movements to carry the gospel to the nations.

SECOND GREAT AWAKENING

The first great wave of students propelled out by revival carried the gospel to the edges of the continents in the early 1800s. More than 20,000 students left their studies, jobs, and families to go to the sailing ships. With limited missionary support and with no assurance they ever would be able to return home, they went to the nations.

This first wave of missionaries primarily evangelized and planted churches on the edges of the lost continents. Limited means of transportation made it impossible to go further.

THE GLOBAL AWAKENING

The second great wave of students carried the gospel to the interiors of the continents in the early 1900s. With improved transportation, these bold students planted churches and evangelized the lost deep inside the continents.

THE THIRD GREAT WAVE

If God should choose to send revival in this day, it is possible that He will call out and launch a third great wave to carry the gospel to the nations. If the first wave impacted the edges of the continents and the second wave impacted the interiors of the continents, where might He send the third wave? Perhaps He will raise up a mighty army of youth and young adults to carry the gospel to the last unreached people groups on earth.

Kingdom Students May Complete the Great Commission

Leaders and parents may get to see their sons and daughters take the gospel to the very last group on earth. And then, according to Scripture, the end will come.

On May 16, 2003, pastor and author John Piper presented a challenge to 30,000 godly collegians sitting in a field in Texas. The students stood to their feet with hands lifted to heaven as Piper gave this powerful closing challenge.

> "When the holiness of God is your passion, you will be a genera-
> tion who lays down your life to fill the earth with His glory.
> For the glory of God's name!
> For the reward of Christ's sufferings!
> In the power of God's Spirit!
> For your everlasting joy!
> For the vindication of God's holiness in the earth!
> In the name of Jesus the Holy One of God!
> Oh, be that generation!"[3]

END NOTES

1. "Speaker: The 'right to be comfortable' an American delusion," *Baptist Press*, July 19, 2004.

2. Mark Matlock. *Generation Hope: Preparing Today's Young People For a Lifetime of Purpose* (Baxter Press, Texas, 2002), 39.

3. Unpublished sermon, OneDay gathering of collegians, May 16, 2003, Sherman, Texas.

Parent Revival and Teaching Suggestions

God always has had a wonderful plan for moving faith down through the generations.

- It always has been God's plan for parents to serve as the primary spiritual influence for their children.
- It always has been God's plan for parents to teach and model truth to their children.
- It always has been God's plan for parents to turn their hearts toward their children so warmth and relationships provide the pipeline for spiritual impact.

Every church leader in the nation knows most church families are not following God's plan. The stakes are so high that slow change seems unacceptable.

- Parenting by many church members is done so poorly that slow change seems unacceptable.
- Spiritual teaching and influence in the homes of many church members is so weak that slow improvement seems unacceptable.
- So few teenagers and collegians are leaving homes with a kingdom focus for their lives that slow change seems unacceptable.

Families don't need incremental change—they need revival! By the power of God, families need dramatic, visible change in a short time. The stakes are too high for business as usual.

Churches that offer parent classes at unpopular hours usually gather a handful of parents. The small group that does respond usually includes some of the best parents who need the least help. Weak parents simply are not being changed by what most churches are offering.

Plan a Parent Revival

A parent revival concentrates the church's prayer and energy on one Sunday. Such a plan provides impact for all parents at the very hours they most likely are present. Here are several principles for planning.

1. *A Parent Revival Should Be Led by the pastor.* The pastor is the spiritual leader of the congregation, and parents look to him for leadership in church and family matters. While many churches have age-group ministers who have special abilities, responsibilities, and training that apply well to parent ministry, the pastor must take the lead. He may enlist and delegate parent training to others, including Christian resource persons from the community; but he should assure the church and any leaders working with parents of his full interest and support.

2. *A Parent Revival Should Be Publicized to Parents in the Church and Community.* Many parents desperately want help and encouragement. Even parents who seem to be effective realize the need for support. Some parents outside the church also are eager for training in parenting skills.

The church should publicize the parent revival to parents inside and outside the church. Church newsletters, bulletins, Web site, and the church marquee are possibilities. Sending news releases to local media can help. Posters for local business displays, flyers for distribution, or a bulk mail campaign can spread the word.

Local schools, day cares, health clubs, doctors' offices, and other family-oriented establishments might make information available to their clients. Finally, church members should personally invite other church members, as well as friends and neighbors who are not church members.

3. *A Parent Revival Should Not End in One Day.* This revival is going to bring conviction, maybe painful conviction, to some parents. Others are going to uncover unresolved problems rooted in their relationships with their own parents. Early on, the church should identify a Christian counselor who can minister to hurting parents with wisdom and compassion.

Other parents will be challenged to follow God in their parenting responsibilities, but they will need encouragement, mentoring, and direction. Other parenting topics (such as single parenting, parenting special needs children, parenting in blended families, etc.) will surface and should be addressed from a loving, biblical perspective. Some parents need help overcoming poor communication skills, ineffective discipline practices, or broken relationships. Such interest may provide ideas for future parent training.

Finally, as parents are revived toward their duties and responsibilities toward God, the church may discover that ministries to preschoolers, children, and students need to change. The church should recognize parents as a child's primary teachers and spiritual leaders. Such discoveries may change ministries, schedules, philosophies, and budgets.

4. *A Parent Revival Must Be Saturated with Prayer.* The only parent revivals that will lead to visible, lasting change in large numbers of families will be those undergirded by a comprehensive prayer strategy. The spiritual leaders of the church should call members to prayer in many different ways before the day arrives. A church might enlist a team of prayer warriors to support the meetings. Ask God to call someone with a deep passion and desire for parent ministry to help lead this prayer effort.

5. *A Parent Revival Should Mobilize the Congregation.* Parent revivals that are staff-planned and staff-executed will not have the power of those involving the full congregation in preparation. A parent revival deserves the same attention that a capital fund-raising campaign receives.

Weeks or months ahead, teams can begin working on prayer strategies, promotion, music, drama, a banquet menu, platform design, and distributing the parenting book to members. Every church will adapt plans appropriate to their unique situations, but most will include these elements focused on parenting:
- Sunday School (with two options below)
- Sunday morning worship (with sample sermon outlines below)
- Sunday evening workshops
- Sunday evening family banquet (during the evening worship time).

Sunday School Option One
The parent revival might begin with all adults in the auditorium for teaching on parenting. In many churches the pastor will lead this session. In other churches, a guest with expertise in family ministry will be invited to lead. The preacher/teacher will shape his instruction to several groups represented in the congregation.
- Those who are parenting.
- Those who plan to parent some day, including collegians and young single adults.
- Those who want to make an impact on their grandchildren.

- Those who are not planning to parent but want to touch the lives of children, including older singles and married persons who cannot have children.

Churches may choose to build the teaching of the day around the book *Parenting with Kingdom Purpose* (Hemphill and Ross, Broadman and Holman Publishers, 2005). Parents will underline material and add their margin notes during each session, creating a valuable resource for future reference. The book is targeted to parents of children, but it also has material for parents of teenagers.

Parenting with Kingdom Purpose clearly communicates:
- God wants children who embody His name, thus reflecting His character.
- He wants children who obey His Word.
- He promises to bless kingdom children so all the nations of the earth might be drawn to Him.

The book is filled with practical instruction in great parenting. Leaders who have been frustrated with weak parenting by church members will be pleased to see those specific issues addressed straightforwardly.

The book also includes instructions for parents who want to teach spiritual truth to their children. As an added bonus, the book includes:
- A salvation and baptism home celebration plan for children.
- A Christian *bar-mitzvah* or *bat-mitzvah* plan for middle schoolers.
- A True Love Waits® home ceremony plan for teenagers.

Many churches will make a video of this service for viewing by those who teach children or teenagers in Sunday School. The video can be shown to these leaders the following Wednesday or Sunday evenings.

Sunday School Option Two

Rather than spotlighting one leader speaking to all adults during Sunday School, other churches will choose a more experiential approach. The following suggestions are designed for such an approach.

TRUTH: A kingdom-focused parent evaluates his or her life in an effort to identify Christlike characteristics and commitments.

FORMAT:

- One-hour seminar for parents during Sunday morning Bible study.
- This session makes use of the personal inventory found in chapter 6 of *Parenting with Kingdom Purpose*, along with additional ideas.
- Parents will be confronted with the authoritative sources describing how children become like their parents.
- The session will help parents understand the dangers their lukewarm spiritual lives present to their children.

PRIOR TO THE SESSION:

1. Provide or sell copies of *Parenting with Kingdom Purpose*.
2. Depending on the meeting area, you may want to enlist some helpers to provide coffee, juice, and simple pastries as parents arrive.
3. For steps 1 and 2, provide paper and pencils or pens.
4. For step 4, provide a marker board or other large pieces of paper and markers.
5. Write the following question on a large sheet of paper or project it on a PowerPoint® slide so everyone in the room can see it: *Is your relationship with God at such a level that you would be happy if your child never rises above it?*

STEP 1. *Think about Matches (5 min.)* Create interest in this session by asking couples or small groups of two or three to create lists of as many matches as possible. Explain that matches are two or more things that are very much alike. (*Examples: socks, cufflinks, bookends, earrings, etc.*) After about two minutes, randomly call for several couples or small groups to share their lists.

STEP 2. *Think about Children and Their Parents (10 min.)* Explain that like the matches just named, research shows us that children are good matches to their parents in several ways. Direct couples or individual parents to list ways their own children are like them. After about four or five minutes, allow some volunteers to read their lists. If you think the group might be reluctant to read their lists aloud, plan to share the list you and your spouse created or preenlist two or three good-natured, confident parents to share their lists. After some sharing, explain that parents often laugh about the physical and personality traits their children have inherited. Focus parents' attention on the fact that children usually rise to the same level of spirituality and Christian commitment they see in their parents.

STEP 3. *Present the Research (15 min.)* Here is an outline to use in presenting research to parents about the development of a child's spiritual life. You may present this information in a way that is most comfortable for you. One such option would be to create a PowerPoint® presentation with each of these points on a slide. Before you begin, tell parents that you will be asking them to think about these points and to determine some of their implications for parenting. Each statement is taken from *Parenting with Kingdom Purpose* and are affirmed by the findings of the National Study of Youth and Religion shared in the chapters of this book.

- By the time they reach young adulthood, the great majority of children will have a faith very similar to their parents' faith. Most parents who want to know where their kids are headed religiously just need to look in the mirror.
- Fact: Six percent of teens see their religious beliefs as very different from their mother's beliefs and just 11 percent say their beliefs differ from those of their father.
- Children tend to become teenagers who believe that God is mostly absent. They tend to think of God only when they have a problem that needs to be addressed. If children tend to have the same faith beliefs as their parents, where does this idea come from?
- Few children rebel against faith in their homes. On the contrary, they tend to think of faith as OK or nice, but it's no big deal. They don't think faith has any great influence on their lives because they don't think anything influences them.
- Many church families think church is important, but not too important. Most churches are losing out to the media and schools for the time and attention of youth. Many parents prioritize homework and extracurricular activities over church attendance. As a result, teens give only a very few minutes to Christian instruction in a week's time.

This is tragic, since children who practice their faith and are involved at church are very different from their peers.

STEP 4. *List the Implications (15 min.)* Move to the marker board or large sheets of paper that you have posted at the front of the room. Encourage parents to name some implications of this research for parenting today. Record their responses on the board or the sheets of paper. Make sure everyone in the room can read the responses and restate each comment so everyone can hear. As time allows, discuss and draw out the deeper meanings from the comments parents make. Conclude this step by stating that while all these facts are true, a greater fact exists: parents are the primary shapers of their children's faith and practice. Direct parents to key Scripture passages that affirm this truth *(example: Deut. 6:4-9)*.

STEP 5. *Parent Checkup (15 min.)* Ask parents to turn to the "Parent Checkup" in *Parenting with Kingdom Purpose*. Explain that the first step to being a kingdom-focused parent is to fearlessly and honestly determine the quality of our own relationship with God. Ask parents to consider this question: **Is your relationship with God at such a level that you would be happy if your child never rises above it?** Display the question so everyone can see it. As the parents work on the "Parent Checkup," remind them that they will not be asked to share this with anyone—although couples or accountability partners may find it helpful to share their checkups with each other. Pray aloud for the group, asking God to speak to their hearts about their own personal relationships with Him.

Sunday Morning Worship Service

The Sunday morning worship service can include "revival quality" music, family testimonies, and preaching. The preacher can give the church a vision for raising children who become spiritually vibrant and kingdom-focused young adults.

Sample Sermon One
THE GOAL OF KINGDOM PARENTING by Ken Hemphill

Text: Luke 2:41-52
How would you like to have a model of effective kingdom parenting? What would be the standards by which we could judge the effectiveness of our parenting?

I can't imagine any parent not wanting to be an effective parent. No one gives birth to a child with the stated purpose of stunting his or her development. Yet many of us do just that because we have been asked to approach one of the most difficult tasks on the planet with little specific training and often without an effective model.

Jesus exemplified the complete kingdom person. Thus we can look to Him for a model of the kingdom-focused person. Further, we might look to His parents for a model of effective kingdom parenting.

1. *The Parent Modeled Kingdom Priority, Luke 2:41-52.* When Jesus was 12, His parents took Him to the Passover in preparation for the day He would become religiously accountable. A Jewish boy became of age on his 13th birthday, so this trip was intended to prepare Jesus for this significant spiritual mile marker.

But a closer look at the context indicates that this was not the extent of the concern Jesus' parents had shown for His spiritual development and kingdom focus. If you look back at 2:21-24, you see that Mary and Joseph had followed the dictates of Scripture at every point. According to the Law of Moses, they brought Jesus to Jerusalem to present Him to the Lord.

While we may not have a ceremony like that in our culture, it is critical that kingdom-focused parents present their children to the Lord. This presentation should be shared with your children as they mature. Tell them you consider them a gift and a stewardship from the Lord.

After they had completed everything according to the law, Mary and Joseph returned to Nazareth. We sometimes read right over a verse that clearly indicates that Jesus' parents continued to model kingdom priorities: *"The boy grew up and became strong, filled with wisdom and God's grace was on Him"* (v. 40). This verse expressly indicates that Mary and Joseph parented in such a way that Jesus grew physically, intellectually, and spiritually. I am particularly drawn to the phrase "God's grace was on Him."

Do your children know that you are as concerned with their spiritual development as you are their physical or intellectual development? Is there ample evidence? Are you as concerned about them memorizing Scripture as you are about their memorizing their multiplication tables? Do you agonize as much about their spiritual diet as you do about their physical one?

Having just read verse 40, I am not surprised to read in verse 41 that Jesus' parents traveled yearly to Jerusalem for the Passover. Their religious devotion—their kingdom focus—was not occasional. It was consistent.

The children of parents with only a nominal commitment to their faith will most often reject that faith. The children at greatest risk today are those whose parents claim to be Christian but have grown casual about their own faith. Jesus grew in God's grace in the context of parents who prioritized His spiritual development.

2. *A Son's Focus on Kingdom Business.* The text and history tell us that pilgrims traveling to Jerusalem often came in large caravans. In many cases, the women and small children went ahead, while the men and older boys followed. Mary and Joseph traveled for a day, each thinking Jesus was with the other or among their relatives. No doubt they looked for Him among the travelers before they returned to Jerusalem. It took them a day to return to Jerusalem and then on the third day they found Jesus.

We really don't need to guess His whereabouts. He was among the teachers in the temple, listening and asking questions. The spiritual hunger nurtured by His parents had created a thirst for spiritual knowledge. Don't miss the impact of verse 47: *"And all those who heard Him were astonished at His understanding and His answers."* Jesus' parents had taught Him God's Word with such care that His knowledge astounded all who heard Him.

His understandably distraught parents asked why Jesus had not been more considerate about their feelings. Jesus' response is worth noting: *"Didn't you know that I had to be in my Father's house?"* (v. 49).

The Greek could actually be translated "about my Father's business." In either case, Jesus' answer indicates that even as a 12-year-old boy He had a clear understanding of the importance of kingdom service. Perhaps His response carries this point. We might paraphrase: "Why are you surprised to find me here? You taught Me that My greatest purpose in life is to advance My Father's kingdom and accomplish His will."

Are you parenting in such a manner that your children know that your greatest desire is that they advance God's kingdom for His glory?

3. *The Obedient Son.* Jesus' answer about His Father's business certainly indicates that He already understood something of His unique relationship to God, His Father. Yet, He willingly submitted to His parents' leadership. He knew this too was the will of His Father in heaven.

Kingdom-focused parenting and the obedience of children go hand in hand. You may recall that in the same context Paul exhorted children to obey and honor their parents (Eph. 6:1-4). He also called upon parents to avoid provoking their children and to bring them up in the training and instruction of the Lord. In other words, parents are to disciple their children. The discipling process will in turn create obedience.

4. *Balanced Development.* Too many children are pressured by parents to develop in only one or two areas of life. Therefore, they do not grow in a balanced manner. In a single verse ripe with meaning (v. 52), we find a summary of the ongoing growth and development of Jesus.

Let's consider the four-fold development of Jesus.
A. WISDOM. Jesus was parented in such a way that He continued to grow in wisdom. His wisdom would have been such that all that He learned would be viewed through the prism of God's Word. Intellectual development must be based on the understanding that all truth emanates from God. Thus, we are responsible for helping our children to develop a Christian worldview. This is essential in our day of relativism.
B. STATURE. Jesus' parents were concerned with His physical development, and a carpenter's trade would have provided a pretty intense physical regimen. If you have ever visited the holy land and driven across some of the areas Jesus visited on foot, you will be awed by the prospect of His physical fitness. During the movie *The Passion of the Christ,* many were moved by the brutal flogging and the agonizing journey to Calvary. Many reflected on the spiritual and physical stamina this moment required.

Our concern for our children's physical development reflects our ultimate desire that they understand that their bodies are the temple of the Holy Spirit (1 Cor. 6:19). Romans 12:1 reminds us that our bodies are the offering we present to the Lord and the context of our spiritual service.
C. FAVOR WITH GOD. Jesus was parented in such a way that nothing discouraged Him from accomplishing the will of His Father. What are you doing to instill in your child this passion to accomplish the will of their Father? Here is where our behavior and priorities must square with our verbal declarations.
D. FAVOR WITH MAN. As Jesus grew, He was highly esteemed and loved by His fellow humans. When Jesus began His public ministry, the inevitable occurred. When He confronted men with their sin and God's

righteousness, they faced a crisis of decision about accepting Him or rejecting Him. Nonetheless, we see Jesus' incredible interpersonal skills. His ability to relate to children, the downcast, the outcast, and the upper caste indicates that His parents had ensured that He had grown in His social skills.

Now we have a model and a goal. We need to disciple our children in such a manner that they will grow intellectually, physically, spiritually, and socially. But the ultimate goal is that our children will make an impact for the kingdom of God.

Sample Sermon Two
WHAT IS A KINGDOM PARENT? by Ken Hemphill

This outline is taken from the book *Parenting with Kingdom Purpose*. Scriptural background for each point can be found there.
1. A kingdom parent has a vital relationship to the King.
2. A kingdom parent is passionate about worshiping the King.
3. A kingdom parent is passionate about prayer.
4. A kingdom parent loves other kingdom people.
5. A kingdom parent encourages the best in others.
6. A kingdom parent sees every event from a kingdom perspective.
7. A kingdom parent seeks first to portray God's righteousness through their behavior and to advance God's kingdom with all their resources.
8. A kingdom parent desires a lifestyle that reflects God's character.
9. A kingdom parent has a passion to study and obey God's Word.
10. A kingdom parent is passionate about reaching the nations.

Sample Sermon Three
"UNLESS THE LORD BUILDS THE HOUSE" by Jerry Drace

Text: Psalm 127:1
Introduction: We buy things we do not want just to impress people we do not like. We build bigger houses for smaller families. We can quote the latest sport statistics, but we forget the birthdays of those who live in our homes. We talk to strangers, but ignore those who share our house. We have two-income families with more debt. We want freedom without re-

sponsibility, education without wisdom, success without sacrifice, religion without righteousness, and marriage without commitment.

We are raising a generation of children with valueless values. Is it any wonder that half of the teenagers who attend church say they are stressed out? More than half say they are confused. Three-fourths say they are looking for answers to the deep questions of life. Fifty-seven percent cannot even say that an objective standard of truth exists.

Tolerance is in. Conviction is out. Personal interpretation is in. Absolute truth is out. It is not that the majority of young people attending church today believe nothing. The problem is they believe everything.

We desperately need a revival in our families today. The word *revival* means, "to live again." This is exactly what needs to take place in our homes. Fathers and mothers need to live again the truths of the Scriptures in front of their children. The family altar needs to be rebuilt or established because a family altar will alter the family.

The text states loud and clear, "Unless the LORD builds a house, its builders labor over it in vain." Five key Scripture passages are centered on the main text. Each one builds on the other.

I. EXODUS 20:5
   A. God Is Jealous
      1. There is a high price to be paid for serving false gods (religion, sports, finances, power, politics, etc.).
      2. The character of the fathers determines the character of future generations.
   B. God Is Merciful
      1. His blessings are on fathers who serve Him and their families.
      2. The greatest gift a husband and father can give his family is to reflect the life of Christ.

II. EXODUS 20:12
   A. Honor Is Earned
      1. Parents need to know that honor, like respect, is received by living a life of integrity in front of your children. What parents do daily speaks louder than what they say on Sunday.
      2. Honor cannot be inherited. Each child must learn it through discipline and obedience, first to God then to parents.
   B. Honor Is Rewarded
      1. The command is to honor your father and mother. A family

should not have two fathers or two mothers. God's plan for a family is very clear in Scripture.

   2. The gift of life is a promise based on the honor children give their parents and the honor they give to God.

III. PROVERBS 3:12

  A. Discipline Proves the Lord's Love

    1. God disciplined David, a man after His own heart.

    2. Jesus corrected Peter, who later preached at Pentecost.

  B. Discipline Proves a Father's Love

    1. Choices bring consequences (rewards or discipline).

    2. Undisciplined children become unruly adults.

IV. 1 TIMOTHY 3:4-5,12

  A. A Personal Note to the Pastor

    1. Take care of your house before you minister in God's house.

    2. Your submission to God's authority sets the example for your children's submission to your authority.

  B. A Personal Note to the Deacons

    1. Be faithful as a partner.

    2. Be fair as a parent.

V. PROVERBS 22:6

  A. Understood Subject

    1. "You" train your own children.

    2. Train their hearts, minds, wills, and consciences.

  B. Understood Expectation

    1. Your children are free to choose your training. They cannot avoid making a choice, though, and they are not free to avoid the consequences of their choices.

    2. Set the example for your children through daily prayer and Bible reading as a family.

Nehemiah 4:14 tells us to fight for our families. There is no greater cause than protecting your family. Surround them with your prayers. Cover them with His Word. Fill them with His promises. Remember, "Unless the LORD builds a house, its builders labor over it in vain."

(Jerry Drace has been in full-time evangelism since 1975. The Jerry Drace Evangelistic Association is located at 236 Sanders Bluff Rd., Humboldt, TN 38343. The Web sites are: *www.jdea.tn.org* and *www.HopefortheHome.org*.)

Sunday Evening Workshops

The gathering on Sunday evening can include separate workshops for:

- parents of preschoolers
- parents of grade schoolers
- parents of teenagers
- parents of college students and young adults
- grandparents
- adults who impact the children of others

Church leaders or special guests should lead specific teaching from *Parenting with Kingdom Purpose* and from this book in relationship to each life situation. During the final 15 minutes, leaders should prepare fathers and other adults to lead family worship at the close of the family banquet.

Sunday Evening Family Banquet

A family banquet is the focus of the evening worship time. The banquet plan might bring back the weak families for Sunday night better than a typical Sunday night service. The evening features wonderful fellowship over a meal, spirited singing, more family skits and testimonies, teaching from the book on parenting, and closing worship.

For this closing worship time, grandparents and adults who want to make an impact on the children of others will move into "family" groups as instructed earlier in the evening. At the same time, intact families circle their chairs and fathers take on the role of spiritual leader by conducting the closing worship. Dads (or moms who head households) learn how to lead this final worship time during the session before the banquet.

Dad gets to try his wings leading out in family worship within the safety of the large group. His children or teenagers might be more likely to respond to him because other families are doing the same thing. Because this first attempt at family worship turns out well, families may be open to the challenge to keep this going for years in their homes.

Conclusion

We don't need incremental change—we need revival. We need a revival in homes that will lead to a full revival in the church and an awakening in our culture.

A Dream for Impacting Teenagers and Their Families

ichard Ross

I have a dream that Christian parents will turn their hearts toward their teenagers.

I have a dream that Christian teenagers—because of warmth and intimacy flowing from their parents—will turn their hearts toward those parents.

I have a dream that parents will spend more time in intercessory prayer for their teenagers.

I have a dream that older teenagers will feel gratitude for all those adults who discipled them, but will sense a special gratitude for their parents who served as their most important disciplers.

I have a dream that parents will feel great appreciation for the church leaders who taught them how to rebuild heart connections and to spiritually lead their teenagers.

I have a dream that parents and teenagers together will make promises of purity to God and will make themselves mutually accountable to each other.

I have a dream that older teenagers will be deeply involved in the ministry of a local church through college and into adulthood because of the impact and example of their parents.

I have a dream that kingdom families will experience vibrant worship, joyful recreation, and rich fellowship planned by church leaders for families.

I have a dream that kingdom families will bring lost and believing teenagers under their roofs for the intentional purpose of influencing them for God.

. I have a dream that kingdom families will bring young believers whose parents are lost (and thus in need of mentors, disciplers, and models of Christian living) under their roofs for the intentional purpose of influence.

. I have a dream that parents will create an anticipation in their children that they will go to the front lines of missions for a substantial time while young—and that parents will begin saving to fund that adventure.

. I have a dream that kingdom families will perform acts of ministry and evangelism together, both locally and internationally.

. I have a dream that teenagers from kingdom families will live primarily to bring honor and glory to the name of God.

. I have a dream that teenagers and collegians from kingdom families will—in God's sovereign timing—lead the church into revival and the culture into a spiritual awakening.

. I have a dream that kingdom parents will champion their teenagers' passion to follow God's clear call, even if that call requires sacrifice and the potential of martyrdom.

ADDENDUM TWO

APPENDIX TWO

Family Dedication at the Birth of a Baby

Richard Ross

(If a ceremony similar to the following were to become common, we would see large numbers teenagers prepared for a major mission adventure while they are young).

PASTOR: This morning I am holding in my arms *(name of child)*, son/daughter of *(p ents)*. Also a part of the dedication of this family today are *(other children present)*. Th baby came into the world on *(date)*. We want to dedicate this family and new chi to God's plans and purposes.

Let me speak first to the parents. If you agree with the following statements, the repeat with "we will."
1. Do you intend to parent in such a manner that your son/daughter will emboc God's name, thus reflecting His character?
2. Do you intend to parent in such a manner that your son/daughter will obe God's Word?
3. Do you intend to parent in such a manner that your son/daughter will take Goc message to the nations?
4. Do you intend to raise your son/daughter in such a manner that he/she will hav a lifelong kingdom focus?

We challenge you to establish a missions adventure savings account for your sor daughter tomorrow. Someday this account will fund your child's extended trip spread the gospel in North America or internationally. Your fellow church membe want to be the first to invest in the future impact of your son/daughter. We a presenting to you a small check that will be used to open the account. As Gc prospers you, we challenge you to add to this amount until all the resources are place by the late high school years.

Let me speak now to the congregation. If you agree with the following statement then answer with "we will."
1. Do you intend to provide love and practical support for this family as they rai their new child?
2. Do you intend to partner with these parents in leading their son/daughter salvation and conformity to the image of Christ?
3. Do you intend to partner with these parents in helping their son/daughter fulf his/her kingdom mission?
4. Do you intend to be prayer warriors for these parents and for this child?

Let me voice one of those prayers right now as I hold this child.